Pr

I DON'T NE__ _____ _

'I absolutely love Toni. She is one of my heroes. So funny and relatable. I didn't read her book though, too busy.'

Christian Hull, author of *Leave Me Alone*

'A nostalgic look back at our Australian childhoods, some questionable life advice and a hilarious explanation as to why Toni is the loveable hot mess she is today. Reading this book felt like hanging out with a best friend.'

Ryan Jon, co-host of the *Toni and Ryan* podcast

'From fits of giggles to unexpected tears, this was like a besties road trip with Toni and a pure delight to read.'

Sarah Davidson, host of the *Seize the Yay* podcast

'Nostalgic, tender, raw and laugh-out-loud funny. I loved it.'

Chrissie Swan, television and radio presenter

'Hilarious, relatable and heartbreaking in equal measure. Toni's words will make you giggle and cry—on repeat.'

Zara and *Michelle* from the *Shameless* podcast

I DON'T NEED THERAPY

(and other lies I've told myself)

TONI LODGE

ALLEN&UNWIN

SYDNEY • MELBOURNE • AUCKLAND • LONDON

This edition published in 2023
First published in 2023

Allen & Unwin
Cammeraygal Country
83 Alexander Street
Crows Nest NSW 2065
Australia
Phone: (61 2) 8425 0100
Email: info@allenandunwin.com
Web: www.allenandunwin.com

*Allen & Unwin acknowledges the Traditional Owners of the Country on which we
live and work. We pay our respects to all Aboriginal and Torres Strait Islander
Elders, past and present.*

A catalogue record for this
book is available from the
National Library of Australia

ISBN 978 1 76106 769 3

Set in 12.75/17.5 pt Minion Pro by Bookhouse, Sydney
Printed and bound in Australia by the Opus Group

15 14 13 12 11 10 9

For Mum

I wish you were alive to read this, but I won't hold it against you

For Taubs

Can you please get some chicken out of the freezer for dinner x

For me

Because I spent a year writing the fucking thing

I don't want to lie to you

Hi! I'm Toni. I know I have 'one of those faces' so you might be wondering where you know me from. You might also be wondering why someone asked me to write a book.

I have a podcast called *Toni and Ryan*, I make funny videos on Instagram and TikTok, I'm a Sagittarius and my favourite food is sandwiches. Saying sandwiches is my favourite food is kind of a cop-out, because you can fill them with other favourite foods. Like, say you love mac and cheese or salad or lasagne? Pop it in a sandwich! I promise there's nothing great that can't be made better by putting it between bread.

I lie to myself constantly about a multitude of little things, like 'that pot needs to soak overnight' or 'my friend will realise they're doing this thing wrong, I don't need to confront them' or 'I will make a healthy Snickers bar with those Medjool dates in the fridge this week!' when the Medjool dates have been in the back of the fridge for three months. Which reminds me, I need to check the best-before date. Maybe I'll make that Snickers bar this weekend . . .

I also lie to other people. Just about little things, like 'no, I don't mind when you make bitchy comments!' or 'dinner out sounds great! Pop me down as a hard maybe' when we all know I'm gonna be knee-deep in salt and vinegar chips and Pepsi Max made in my SodaStream.

We all tell ourselves lies like that, but it wasn't until I sat down to write this book that I realised it wasn't just the little things I was lying to myself about, but the big stuff too. Things like, 'I'm really happy for that friend' when they excelled at something I wanted to excel at, or 'I'm too fat to do that' when whatever the thing was didn't have a weight limit, or 'I can get through this' when I found out my mum had cancer.

• • •

Sometimes, it feels like life is full of only right and wrong, only black and white—but this isn't that. This is the grey area. Of course, there are also parts of this book that are blue and green and sparkly, but I wanted to include the grey parts too. They are the bits of a story that don't make the cut when you retell it at a cocktail party or when you meet your partner's parents for the first time.

I don't like confrontation, so this is my version of it: exposing myself to you in this book, in a way where you see those grey parts and how shit they've been, but also how they've made the colourful parts even shinier. In each chapter, I'll show you a different part of my life, and every part will bring a new lie. You'll read the big lies and the little lies, and we'll delve into the reasons the world is *definitely* against me. I will also dispense some unsolicited advice which I am authorised to share because I am writing a book and no one can stop me.

But hey, full disclosure—this isn't self-helpy, it doesn't end in some 'EUREKA!' moment where I tell you how to have the perfect life or how to style a capsule wardrobe (what the fuck is that?) or whatever.

This is just me—no punchline.

Without further ado—here are the truths I've learned about myself through the lies I've told.

Love ya,

Toni

I don't want to be famous,
part one

When I was a tiny girl—and by tiny I mean in age, not body shape—I remember telling my mum and anyone else I could get to listen to me that I would be famous. It didn't matter that I was just a chubby girl from Roleystone.

I have told so many people that I've always thought I'd be famous, and when they ask why, I simply say, 'I just knew it. It's the Lodge Magic.'

'What's the Lodge Magic?!' I hear you cry from across the bright blue yonder. Well, the Lodge Magic is something I made up.

• • •

I existed in this perfect, privileged life. I had two loving parents who loved the heck out of me and each other. I had three siblings, my brother, Jamie, my sister Libby and my sister Hayley. They are all way older than me (thirteen, eleven and ten years older, respectively), which I have always thought is so cool. They would always buy me the sickest birthday presents and take me to awesome places because they all worked and had their licences. It was kind of like having one set of older, more nurturing parents and one set of younger, cooler parents.

In 1998, when *Mulan* came out, I was five, and Jamie took me to see it at the Hoyts Cinema at Carousel in Cannington. I was so excited about it all week and carefully chose an outfit and how to wear my hair.

Knowing what I know about money now, I realise that Jamie probably wasn't earning that much—but he never spared a dollar on me. He bought tickets, a massive box of popcorn, a large Coke for himself and a small lemonade for me. Being five years old, I wasn't allowed to drink Coca-Cola. My parents were pretty laid back, but I wasn't allowed Coke—did anyone else have that? It feels like such a weird line to draw, thinking about it now.

We wandered into the cinema to watch the previews, sitting right at the front, where the carpet was the least sticky and I could see the whole screen—and you couldn't wipe the smile off my face. My cool older brother, who could drive and was RICH, was with me, at the cinema, seeing the movie of the year!

When you're an excited five-year-old, you can't pace yourself. Handfuls and handfuls of popcorn went into my body before the lights even turned off, and the buttery, salty goodness left me positively parched, so I sucked up all of my lemonade to wash it down. The movie started and I was loving it sick. I was continuing to mindlessly insert popcorn into the hole in my face, when I got one of the brown husky bits stuck in the back of my throat and started to choke. Naturally, I panicked. I reached for my lemonade, but it was empty. I was coughing so much that I didn't even hear how 'I'll Make a Man Out of You' ends.

Jamie started rubbing my back and offered me a sip of his Coke. I responded in a whisper-yell, 'I'm not allowed Coke!' while still coughing and ruining the cinema experience for other patrons. Jamie insisted, so finally I caved and had some Coke, completely solving the problem and leaving us able to move on with the rest of our lives.

After the movie, we talked about how much we'd loved it. When we got in the car, Jamie warned me I couldn't tell Mum that I'd had Coke. I was rattled. I didn't lie to Mum! Mum was the perfect angel of my life. But I realised we had only been given one rule, and it had been broken, and what if she didn't let me go to the cinema again?!

I started to sweat. I remember Jamie saying, 'You actually don't have to say anything about it—don't say, "I didn't have Coke", you just don't have to mention it.'

The closer we got to home, the more nervous I became. We walked into the house and Mum had the biggest smile on her face, excited to ask us how we enjoyed the movie.

She got halfway through saying, 'Hey Tone, how was the movie?' before I exploded.

'JAMIE GAVE ME COKE!'

Mum looked quite shocked, actually. Jamie probably rolled his eyes and explained my near-death experience.

• • •

So, yes, I grew up with siblings who beat me up and bullied me in the loving way siblings do, like when Hayley tricked me into asking Mum for things that she would also benefit from, such as Caramello Koalas or a PlayStation 1. Or Libby conning me into opening the front gate for her and doing other stupid tasks by saying she would time me. But then they all got older and moved out, and I got to be an only child for a while. I honestly had the best of both worlds. Even though they've always called me a brat for being spoiled, they're just jealous that I'm the favourite. (Cue texts from each sibling, arguing that they're the favourite. I know they're reading this because I forced them all to buy a copy.)

I didn't have to make any conscious decisions in my bubble. It wasn't until I was older that I had to start making really difficult choices and taking chances, and realised the very existence of the safety net I'd grown up with.

I never had to worry about running out of money. I never lost sleep over my phone bill or paying for car insurance or needing to manage my finances properly at all, because my parents were always able to help me out. Like I said, very privileged, and I know lots of people don't have that. I was given the gift of not needing to worry about the big stuff—plus the Lodge Magic, which would take care of anything else.

7

When reflecting on my life up until this point, anytime someone has said, 'Whoa, Toni, you're so unlucky!', I've responded with the fact that some bad things have happened, but I've always scraped through by the skin of my teeth. Like it's sometimes been something as small as our dinner reservation being cancelled at the last minute, and our backup option leading to an amazing discovery—or something more dramatic like when I was in a really bad car accident and walked away without a scratch. *It's the Lodge Magic.*

• • •

When I started going to uni, I had a red 2003 three-door Hyundai Getz (not sponsored) and still lived at home, which was the same position most of my friends from school and work were in. At uni, I met friends who lived out of home, didn't have a car their Mum and Dad paid for, ate canned beans and could only afford one jug of beer and the kind of cigarettes you had to roll yourself.

One of those friends, Taubs, turned out to be the love of my life.

Taubs is the calmest person I've ever met. He's very cool and laid back, all the things that are the polar opposite to loud, obnoxious, love-to-have-the-room me.

Taubs is a quiet achiever. He's so quippy and so clever, you don't realise he's made a joke or proved you wrong until it's too late and the conversation has moved on, and you'd look even more stupid if you brought it up again—but he's also so caring that he'd never want to make you feel stupid.

We were both studying sound engineering, and he helped me with my homework and gave me advice on shows I was working on. He was lovely and special and so tall. But he couldn't drive (and he still can't) so I started picking him up for uni here and there, or driving him home, and we got along great.

One day, long before we became kissing friends, I was being a fuckhead with no shoes on and got glass in my foot in the uni theatre. I started to panic and he grabbed my shoulders, sat me down and looked me dead in the face, saying, 'You need to not panic. This is totally fine. Take three deep breaths.' He then turned on his phone torch and plucked the glass out. Something about him touching my disgusting feet to help me stop panicking made me feel so special.

Finding Taubs is the biggest example of Lodge Magic there has ever been in the universe.

But lots of things in my life felt like they came down to that specific magic feeling, and I would give the Lodge Magic credit where, looking back, it wasn't deserved. Like was it really the Lodge Magic that made Taubs and me fall in love? Or are we just two great people who have similar values and get along really well? Is it really the Lodge Magic that led to me writing this book, right now, in my dressing gown? It drives Taubs crazy in two ways—he thinks the magic isn't the only thing hard at work here, and he is frustrated by the inexplicable way the magic takes care of things.

I always thought I was the only one lucky enough to have the Lodge Magic—until one day my brother, Jamie, was in a particularly sticky situation, where something he had ordered for work wasn't going to arrive before it needed to be shipped off (or something), which is where the magic works best! In sticky, but usually non-life-threatening situations. I remember saying, 'What are you going to do, Jam? How are you going to get yourself out of this?'

And he said, 'Toni . . . it's the Lodge Magic.'

I looked at Taubs, who rolled his eyes. Then I shot a look at my sister-in-law Chelsea, who shook her head. I turned back to my brother with the cheekiest expression.

It's just the Lodge Magic.

• • •

After telling anyone and everyone who might possibly listen about how famous I'd be, it became an obsession and something I leaned on heavily.

I'd look at schoolwork and think, 'Pfft I don't need this shit,' because I'd be famous when I was older! I didn't need to know the value of x and y, my accountant could deal with that and just let me know how many yachts I could afford. I'd think about jobs I wanted to apply for, and daydream about how those jobs would lead to my fame and fortune. I'd get tickled with thoughts of singing to myself in a public toilet and being confronted by a woman with fiery red hair styled in a French roll wearing a pants suit, who would smash the lock off the door and demand that I join her music label and perform in a last-minute arena concert, like in *The Lizzie McGuire Movie*. There just wouldn't be a situation I'd be in where I didn't think about how it could change my future in some crazy, unforeseen way.

My potential whirlwind careers changed a lot. They went from going on *Australian Idol* and getting a record deal with Sony BMG and being a famous singer, to being First Flute in the West Australian Symphony Orchestra, to being an improv comedy actor like Rebel Wilson in *The Wedge*, to being a prima ballerina for the Australian Ballet (WHY DIDN'T ANYONE TELL ME THAT WOULDN'T HAPPEN? I HAVE NO TRUE FRIENDS), to being an opera singer.

Then came a long period starting when I was seventeen where I thought I'd lost the Lodge Magic, and I kissed my dreams goodbye. I'd gotten so used to things happening quickly, that the second something took 'too long' to happen, I just assumed that was it. I'm very impatient. I truly thought I'd work in the Coles deli for my whole life.

Don't get me wrong, I loved my time in the Coles deli. Doesn't everyone have that job when they're at uni or school that they hate at the time, but look back on so fondly? That was mine. I worked with two of my best friends from school, Alex and Lauren. We'd spray each other with the hose and slip over and sing songs about chickens. But I didn't want to work there forever.

Just after I'd enrolled for another year at university, the Lodge Magic returned in the shape of a part-time job loading the audio for commercials at a radio station in Perth. Basically it was an admin position, with some audio cutting and recording thrown in for good measure. I would be like a spare audio floater. Instantly, the pictures in my brain changed from me slicing honey ham and cleaning chicken stuffing off the inside of those massive industrial deli ovens to me making a joke in the office kitchen and someone saying, 'TONI! YOU'RE A NATURAL! Hamish and Andy can't go on, are you able to step in for the day?!'

And actually, that's kind of what happened.

(It's not.)

· · ·

I have been offered every job I've ever had an interview for. Every single one! (Who is that good? Must be the Lodge Magic!)

Except for one.

And it just so happens it was the one that I thought would finally put me on my path to fame and success and pure ecstasy (the feeling, not the drug).

I interviewed for this job and made the best fucking production reel I'd ever created. I used my shiniest personality and told my funniest jokes and casually expressed (lied) about how much I loved the station—and I didn't get it.

RADIO'S OFF. WE'RE OFF RADIO. NOT HAPPENING. BACK TO COLES WE GO.

You might be surprised to read at this point that I *overreacted*.

Because, about a week later, I got a call from the guy who was hiring for the role I didn't get, Carl (keep reading, he redeems himself). He'd heard of a similar job in Bunbury, which is around an hour and 40 minutes south of Perth, except I'd be making radio commercials and working full time. Meaning I'd have to move my whole life away from my friends, family and boyfriend.

I've already told you I've only been turned down for one job I've interviewed for, so yep! I got the job in Bunbury and started making radio ads full time for $40K a year.

I'd actually just moved out of home and into a house with Taubs, so this cool new life I had was about to be over, but I was so happy and excited. The dream of being called on-air at the last minute and becoming a radio star after cracking a joke about a tin of tuna in the work kitchen became a possibility once more.

The next little while was a bit of a blur. Settling into a new city, learning a new job and driving the three-and-a-bit-hour round trip to kiss Taubs on the mouth every SINGLE weekend.

Then I suddenly started on-air in the way most radio stars do: handing out cans of Coke (which I was *finally* allowed to drink!) and cartons of chocolate milk from a radio station car. I was a last-minute fill-in when someone was sick, and I drove around the south-west saying, 'HEY, IT'S TONI WITH THE HIT SQUAD DOWN AT THE SOUTH WEST SPORTS CENTRE. I'VE GOT HARVEY FRESH ORANGE JUICE, OAK FLAVOURED MILK AND ICE BREAK ICED COFFEE.'

I'm aware I just said *saying* and then typed that in all capitals. I was so nervous that when the breakfast show would call me to do my live-cross on the radio, I would scream it down the phone in ten seconds flat instead of sounding hot, cool and like a person someone would actually want to find in public and trust to take a drink from.

I give you: the beginning of my on-air career.

• • •

While I was settling into my job, I was learning more and more about the radio industry. Like how things worked, what every department actually did and how to climb the non-corporate ladder. I had no idea it was its own universe, or that the people I had teaching me, mentoring me and becoming my lifelong friends were people that other radio hopefuls would kill for ten minutes with. While brushing up on the industry, I started to just devour any radio information I could get my hands on and learn about any and all radio shows. That included a drive show from New Zealand called *Jase & PJ*.

The first *Jase & PJ* video I ever watched was the one where PJ says she lies on the couch with her cousin, but it's 'okay because his partner is there too' and Jase laughs and says that's why he always lies and tells her he's busy when she invites him over.

I couldn't believe how funny it was. Two hours passed and I'd watched every single *Jase & PJ* video, scoured both of their personal Instagram accounts and licked the *Jase & PJ* yoghurt pot (figurative yoghurt pot, that is) clean. I was a woman obsessed! By this time Taubs had moved down to Bunbury to live with me, and as a treat, every afternoon at five o'clock, when they'd post another video from their show, Taubs and I would watch the latest video on the couch together and piss ourselves laughing. They would laugh and joke together like genuine best friends, and they would always rag on each other and their team like family. It was like watching genuine happiness.

In early November, a few months after I'd first come across the show, the stars aligned: Jase and PJ were moving to Australia and doing a breakfast radio show in Melbourne! My dream radio show and dream city, and they were hiring for my job!

Once again, I got on the tools and whipped up the slickest and shiniest version of every radio promo I'd ever made, along with a cover letter that would make you think I had personal investment in the interests not only of the show, but of Jase and PJ as human beings. I began to imagine going for coffee with PJ after a yoga class on a Sunday morning. I daydreamed about sitting at the pub with Jase. I saw myself in their videos, making them laugh the way they did me.

And I didn't get the job. Didn't even get an interview.

(Technically, this doesn't *actually* count towards my shiny interview-to-job record, right? I didn't get the interview, so I think I still have a near-perfect record.)

Immediately, I was off radio again. I couldn't believe they'd let an opportunity to work with me slip through their fingers. I lied to myself, and to Taubs, saying, 'Maybe they aren't even that funny.'

He said, 'Fuck off they aren't. You didn't get the job and that's okay.'

But I didn't think it was okay.

I was getting ready to leave work on a Monday afternoon a few weeks later, in early December, when I got an email from the head of production at a radio station called KIIS in Sydney and Melbourne (for those who are playing at home, YES, the same station Jase and PJ were moving to). He wanted to have a chat, and asked if I was available at 9 a.m. the next day.

I immediately responded. 'Of course—whenever suits you!', knowing full well that 9 a.m. for him was 6 a.m. for me. I was disappointed that I wouldn't be able to go to the gym before work. 'I'll go afterwards instead,' I lied to myself.

The next morning at 6 a.m., my phone buzzed with this new opportunity. The production head explained to me that the job at *Jase & PJ* had been filled, but they liked what I sent them and wanted to know if I'd like to interview for a totally different job in Sydney, where I'd be working on a night show instead of breakfast radio.

I played it cool and said, 'That could be alright.'

Inside, I was thinking, WOW, WHAT, SYDNEY?! (Actually, if you ask that guy on the phone, Boz, he would probably confirm I didn't play it cool and I definitely sounded excited.)

Taubs was away working at the time, so I called him excitedly with the news and then immediately undercut myself with, 'Nothing will probably come of it, but what a great contact to make!'

But by that Friday afternoon, I was calling Taubs again, this time to ask if it was okay if we moved from Bunbury to Sydney because I'd been offered the job.

He responded, 'Yeah, mate, of course. We can figure it out. Now, I've gotta go and tune this band, we're on in fifteen minutes.'

• • •

It was probably the most stressful few weeks of my life, to be honest. It wasn't sexy and it wasn't simple. We had to sell almost everything we owned, and fit all of the essentials into my Toyota Yaris—which my brother Jamie managed to get put on a truck and sent to Sydney for me by calling in a few favours. And to add a little bit more fun, time-based pressure, we had already planned (and paid) to spend Christmas in Japan with friends, so it was fucking go time. When we got to Sydney, we had to live in an Airbnb for like six weeks because we couldn't find (or afford) a good rental in Sydney.

At KIIS, I was working on a night show called Celeb HQ. For six months, I worked, learned and hustled, while still watching the latest *Jase & PJ* videos on my dinner breaks and lusting over what might have been. During my time in Sydney, I met a gangly dork called Franco at a house party. I wasn't very interested in talking to him until someone told me he worked at *Jase & PJ*. I didn't play it cool whatsoever, asking, 'IS PJ AS COOL IN REAL LIFE AS SHE SEEMS?!'

He nervously responded, 'Yes, she is.'

In that moment, I decided maybe Franco wasn't so bad after all. I asked him if he thought I could ever get a job at *Jase & PJ* and he responded, 'No way, it's such a great show! Everyone there is there for good, I think.'

'Pfft. Nothing is that good,' I lied to myself.

About a week later, a job ad went up for the very same role at *Jase & PJ* I'd applied for six months prior. Without a moment's hesitation, I sprinted into my boss's office and said, 'I know I haven't been here for long, but you'd be insane not to give me that job with Jase and PJ!'

One week later, Taubs and I signed a lease on an apartment in Richmond in Melbourne. I started my new job at *Jase & PJ* at 4.30 a.m. the following day.

The Lodge Magic.

• • •

The job at *Jase & PJ* seemed like sunshine and rainbows, fun and fame and excitement—and it really, truly was.

Taubs and I drove from Sydney to Melbourne, staying over-night in Albury with an old friend from radio in Bunbury, and we arrived in Melbourne at 9 a.m. the next morning.

I went into the radio station to meet everyone I'd be working with on the show. Taubs stayed in the car, extremely hungover, and waited for me with all of our precious belongings.

The team were busily working away before the weekend. Everyone was absolutely lovely—except PJ. The new yoga-and-coffee friend I'd dreamed of was acting really rude and horrible to me, and to everyone on the team, and my heart shattered into a million pieces.

I began questioning everything. I'd quit my job! I'd moved my life to Melbourne on a whim because of some funny videos on the internet! What would we do for money? I'd been catfished! TAUBS WAS IN THE CAR DOWNSTAIRS WITH ALL OF OUR BELONGINGS!

As my mind raced through the mistakes I'd made, tears streamed out of my eyes and I couldn't believe what I'd done to my family of two.

Then everyone burst out laughing, ran over to comfort me, gave me a massive group hug and screamed 'WELCOME TO THE TEAM!' I realised it was a prank—the first of many—and knew I was now part of the family.

The path to yoga, coffee and fame was clear ahead.

• • •

Very early in my time at *Jase & PJ*, I sit down with PJ one night after too many non-virgin cocktails, and she asks me who I want to be and where I want to go.

It's a hard question to answer, isn't it?

Lately, my Lodge Magic has been working overtime and it occurs to me that it might be too cocky to ask for even more. Even so, I say, 'I want to be famous.'

PJ asks, 'Why do you want to be famous? What is it about fame that you actually want?'

With those two simple questions, the ambitions I've had for my whole life start to crumble. The truth is, I'm not really sure what I want out of fame—if I want people to know my name or to never be able to go to a Coles and do my own food shopping for fear of being papped, or to be rich. All I know is I've promised my mum and every single person I've ever met that that's what I'd be: famous.

I think PJ realises she's asked a life-altering question, and scrambles, saying, 'I think you need to change your definition of fame! You don't need to be famous—you just need to find somewhere where you can be you.'

And I start to realise that's all it is. I want a job where I'm able to crack jokes and make videos and have fun and share my story and be able to support myself with those parts of me—and to leave behind the ham-slicing.

I loved my time at *Jase & PJ*—I found my voice and my confidence and realised what my dream truly was. I got to do funny radio stunts and make stupid videos and make people laugh and I could have never dreamed of that being my day to day.

Riding an electric scooter to buy sausage sizzles from Bunnings and having to carry them back in my little basket, running through the airport and getting escorted out by security, having skittles sprayed in my face with a leaf blower, sprinting through the city carrying trays of beer to bring back to the studio, singing opera to Meghan Markle and Prince Harry—it beat any nine-to-five job, at least the kind Dolly Parton was singing about.

Learning I could be me and that, for the first time in my life, knowing that was more than enough. Just me.

• • •

The last year or so has been a really wild time. I've been making people laugh, making stupid videos, WRITING A BOOK and making a podcast that people AROUND THE WORLD listen to when they're feeling glum. For that chubby little girl from Roleystone who told her mum she'd be famous, that is absolutely insane. But for my mum not to see it is really hard.

As I'm writing this, the lump in my throat is rising and I'm wishing that this was one of the lies. I wish so hard that this wasn't part of the book and I could say, 'Hey Siri, call Mum' and my mum would actually be the person who answered. But that's not the case.

I've pinkie-promised myself that I'd see everything my mum wanted to but couldn't, and what better way for her to see it than through the eyes of her grown-up (still chubby) daughter living the best life in the fucking world?

◎

Reasons the world is against me— pedestrian crossings

I don't like people who are rude. I'm loud and obnoxious, which is different from rude. I'd never be rude to someone. Even if there was a reason, I'd probably say approximately sixteen horrible things in my head then smile far too wide and be over-the-top polite. Actually, that's probably also pretty rude . . .

Okay, I'll reassess.

I hate inconveniencing people. I never want to be the reason someone is late or put out or thrown off schedule. I'm irritatingly early and always organised. Need a pen? I have three. Got a scratchy throat? Have a Strepsil. Accidentally met a cat and need an antihistamine? You know I've got some Claratyne in my bag.

Unfortunately, I hold others to the same standard. I find lateness incredibly disrespectful, and someone rocking up to a meeting and saying, 'Does anyone have a pen I could borrow?' sends shivers down my spine quicker than stepping into a walk-in freezer.

Is this expectation unfair? Absolutely. Can I stop it? No. If I can make things run like clockwork, then why can't others? I'd never intentionally inconvenience someone else, so WHY do other people do it to ME? It seems only fair, doesn't it?

This brings me to something that sends me to boiling point almost daily: pedestrian crossings.

No one likes being stuck in traffic. It's claustrophobic, frustrating and a waste of time. With all of that in mind, who would EVER make being stuck in traffic worse? These people.

In Australia, pedestrian crossings use push-buttons, where a pedestrian pushes a button to alert the system that it needs to stop the flow of car traffic so they can cross. Basically, the button stops cars by changing the traffic light from green to red.

Now, people who push the button, stop the traffic and cross happily and safely with their dog/baby/shopping trolley/whatever aren't the problem.

Here's the problem: people who push the button and then run across the road when it's quiet instead of waiting for the lights to change. They deserve a fine. People who press the button and then walk on by deserve to be jailed.

YOU CAN'T PRESS THE BUTTON AND FUCK THE FLOW OF TRAFFIC FOR NO REASON. And before anyone sends me hate mail about how that's not how it works—yes it is.

I don't care if this seems like a massive overreaction, it is disrespectful and incredibly frustrating. Just the other day, I was driving to work to record the podcast. I was not running late, despite heavy traffic (I had obviously built a buffer of fifteen minutes into my journey), but it was getting close. I was at a three-way intersection in my little hatchback, probably listening to Lorde, when I saw a group of youths hit EVERY pedestrian crossing button, and then KEEP ON WALKING in the other direction.

They had no need to hit even ONE of the buttons, but they did it, and added probably an extra three to four minutes to my journey. FOR NO REASON.

This proves that the world is against me. I am a victim and I would like to campaign to introduce enforceable fines for people pressing buttons WILLY-NILLY.

I don't need therapy, part one

In Western Australia, part of our primary school curriculum is swimming lessons. It makes sense because it's so fucking hot and every second house has a swimming pool—I guess also because the whole state is basically a beach—but while practical, it's definitely a form of torture. 'You want me to wear my BATHERS in front of the OTHER KIDS and then get changed in front of ALL the other girls, and then sit in the classroom with wet hair for the rest of the day? EXCUSE ME?'

Yet this would happen every single year for two weeks.

These swimming lessons began in Year 3. I'm a very good swimmer, so I refuse to believe (even now, in my late twenties) that I had to go. It's definitely Department of Education–approved torture. You'd rock up to school wearing your bathers under your uniform, carrying your school bag and another, separate bag (usually a plastic shopping bag) with your towel, goggles, sunscreen and spare knickers.

Probably relevant here: I was *not very popular* as a kid. It may seem hard to believe now, but when I was a child, I didn't do too well socially. I was chubby and not particularly well liked, and hadn't yet had the opportunity to figure out the stellar personality and charisma I developed later. Like, it was fine and I'd have friends here and there, but for the most part, I would eat lunch on my own or be a bit of a group floater. I know that when I say 'group floater', someone from your primary school or workplace will come to mind. Probably someone nice and harmless, but not really best friend material? That was me.

I think I'm having some kind of breakthrough right now and realising I'm not best friend material and that feels like something I should file away and talk to my therapist about.

Anyway. Back to the first day of lessons in Year 3. I rocked up to school with my plastic bag of towel/goggles/knickers/sunscreen and walked to the bus to go to swimming before realising we had to ride with some of the bigger kids.

Catching the bus for a field trip or swimming or camp as a kid is interesting. You always have to partner up. EVERY TIME! As someone who wasn't best friend material, I always struggled on this front. Most of the other kids had that person whose arm they'd automatically grab the moment the teacher told us we had to pair up, while I'd either be forced into a pairing with someone I didn't like (or, more commonly, who didn't like me) or be the odd one out.

We walked onto the bus and saw that the bigger kids had staked their claim on the good seats, while some naughty boys had already been split up so they were sitting on their own seats. We piled onto the bus, two by two, except for me. I realised my fate of sitting next to a naughty older boy who would definitely bully me, given the chance.

'No, no, no, no, no,' I thought. 'Why is this happening to me?'

I got this funny, hot, sick feeling in my tummy as I got plonked down next to the naughty older boy. He made a totally unfunny joke about not having enough room on the seat if I was sitting next to him, and the mate he'd been separated from laughed from across the way, then shouted 'EWW! Whose parachute is that?'

It was my parachute. He was pointing at my plastic bag, from which my pink frilly knickers from Kmart were sticking out of the top.

Everyone laughed (okay) and laughed (cool). I poked the pink frilly knickers down to the bottom of my bag. The funny, hot, sick feeling got worse and the bus took off.

To this day, my knickers go at the very bottom when I'm packing a bag. I know—tell me you have trauma without telling me you have trauma.

• • •

When I was in Year 4, we had a free dress day. For anyone not familiar, in Australia basically every school has a uniform. Some are more laid back and chill, like a school polo shirt and whatever else you want on the bottom as long as it's the right colour, and some are very full-on, like ironed shirt, tie, blazer, skirt and stockings. A free dress day was when the school would con you into making a gold-coin donation by saying you could wear your own clothes.

Free dress day was a big deal in the calendar. It was one of the few days you could show off your cool weekend clothes or wear your hair down. It was a school year highlight.

Cast your mind back to 2002 and imagine this: wide-leg, three-quarter denim shorts from Piping Hot, white and blue Gallaz shoes, a bright orange Maui and Sons T-shirt and a light blue, fleecy, zip-through Columbia jacket. I'd probably got Libby to curl or crimp my hair as well. *Pretty. Cool.*

My mum dropped me off at school (at the crosswalk—that was the cool place to get dropped off, because you had to walk across the road to get to school, like a real grown-up). I had my backpack on, a single two-dollar coin in my sweaty little palm to donate to Jeans for Genes. I strutted my way into the schoolyard (ten minutes early, of course) knowing I looked cool as fuck and would probably get home from school with twelve boyfriends.

That's when I started to see some kids running around, all in uniform.

'Losers,' I thought to myself. 'They've forgotten about free dress day. Their mums mustn't love them like mine does.'

Then I saw more and more kids who had their uniforms on, and I quickly noticed that I was the odd one out. The funny, hot, sick feeling returned as I realised it was me. ME. I'M THE ONE STANDING OUT. And for anyone paying attention, it was pretty hard not to stick out in the sick ensemble I'd decided on for the day. My strut turned into a power walk across the basketball courts to my classroom to hide out. I cried on Ibu Wishart's lap (Mrs Wishart, who was also the Indonesian teacher) and never wanted to be seen again. I stayed at school all day in free dress and cried my eyes out when my mum picked me up, and I probably said something horrible, like how she didn't love me.

· · ·

When I was in Year 5, I had a teacher who I liked fine, but his favourite subject was maths, which was definitely *not* my area of expertise. I've always loved music, words and language (which I guess is why I'm writing a book and not making a fucking calculator) and I don't think he loved that I was a bit more arty-farty than I was into numbers.

It's every teacher's aim to get their students to love learning and feel passionate about what they're passionate about and I COMPLETELY respect that. I've always tried to make the people around me care about what I do every day, and try to show them why I love it—and that's fine.

But I don't like being pushed. I like to make my own choices and have (the impression of) autonomy. To this day, when someone pushes or challenges me or backs me into a corner, I feel indignant about it, even if it's about something I'm already planning to do. Like when you're about to do the dishes and then someone says, 'Hey, do you mind doing the dishes?' and you're like, 'Fuck off, now I don't wanna do it'? Kind of like that.

When it came to this teacher, I would get that funny, hot, sick feeling in my tummy every time he would bring up maths. And as teachers do, he would call on me in class a LOT to try to get me excited about the subject. I used to daydream a fair bit in that class and that really fucked him off as well (fair enough).

I would often go to the sick bay, and Mrs Hunt in the office would call my mum to come and rescue me. My mum was a wonderful and caring woman. However, having to come and pick me up EVERY WEEK at the same kind of times made her pretty angry (also fair enough). She and my dad owned a business, so whenever she would have to come and pick me up, she would lose a heap of time she could have spent at work. As a working adult now, I can only imagine how fucking annoying it was.

You can probably see where this is going. The familiar funny, hot, sick feeling in my tummy would come when I was in class, so I wanted to get the hell out of there. But then, when Mrs Hunt had to call my mum, the funny, hot, sick feeling in my tummy would get worse. But it would also get worse if I sat in class. A real rock-and-a-hard-place kind of situation.

I would learn later that there's a name for that feeling: anxiety. Anxiety and I would become well acquainted beyond this time, and not just when I was on the bus or in maths class.

• • •

In Year 10, my high school stopped offering music as a subject, and that was a deal-breaker for me. I'd been taking lessons in flute and piano, I was part of the concert band, I was in the choir—I was basically Mozart. So I moved to a new school with a great music program, and was so nervous that I don't think I slept for about three months before I started.

I moved from a school where I'd known most of the kids since we were five and crying when we were getting dropped off by our parents, to a new school where everyone else knew everyone else and I was *very* aware of it. I was also coming from the pretty laid-back world of public education to a private school with a very strict uniform. On days where we had sport lessons, we had to bring a separate duffel bag with our sport clothes and shoes in it. Very annoying.

On my first day, my mum dropped me off and I found out there were only two other girls starting new in Year 10, but they were thin and sporty and quite cool. I realised very quickly that their school-moving experience would probably be fairly different from mine. (It was.)

This new school was far from my house and Mum and Dad both worked, so I had to get myself there. I had grown up walking to and from school and, all of a sudden, I had to catch not one, but TWO buses—and boy howdy, was that not the most anxious I had ever felt.

My second day was the first time I caught the bus. I talked myself into it, put my iPod earphones in and was very brave.

It also happened to be a sports day, so I had my entire outfit change in my second bag. The first bus wasn't too bad. There were lots of kids from all different schools, so I didn't really stick out because no one knew who I was anyway. The second bus was one of those long stretchy buses with two parts. I panicked while boarding—the bus was a lot fuller than I'd anticipated—but I decided to commit to the last seat of the front of the bus, next to a boy who seemed harmless.

We arrived at school and got off the bus and a very cool girl with long blonde hair who always wore sunglasses told me I'd sat next to a real dork and that was lame.

I instantly became hot and red and said, 'I don't care about that, I just wanted a seat,' while in my head I was panicking and saying, 'PLAY IT COOL, DON'T CRY, IT'S FINE,' as she walked off.

Having grown up walking to school, I hadn't understood the hierarchy of the back and front of the bus: the front is for losers and the back is for cool kids. If you committed to the back of the bus, you'd better be cool enough to sit there. If you weren't, you'd get laughed right off the bus and might as well change your name.

I attempted to unscramble my brain from my bus faux pas and rushed into school. I was on the edge of tears when, thankfully, the Lodge Magic struck. My homeroom teacher, Miss Dewar, was also the head of music. Knowing that I would face someone with a love for art just like mine every single morning, I finally felt safe.

My first lesson was sport, so I walked up to the sports centre, duffel bag in hand, before clocking that everyone around me had their duffel bag straps over their shoulders, and were wearing them like backpacks. I very *casually* attempted to not stick out by slipping the bag across my back.

I was standing out the front of the sports centre with about 80 other kids when a teacher walked out and shouted, 'COME WITH ME IF YOU'RE IN MY CLASS!' Well, what fucking help was that? I didn't know who the teacher fucking was!

The hot feeling rose in my tummy and the tears knocked again. I got soft and wobbly, and a girl standing near me noticed that I was probably about to soak into the floor and asked, 'Who do you have?'

I yanked out my timetable and stuttered out that I had Miss Stone. This lovely girl pointed her out and I wandered inside.

As all dorks who are on the edge of hysterical crying do, I sat at a desk in the middle of the front row of the class. The kids who had friends already occupied the back rows. A cool group of girls walked in. There were five of them. In the front row of desks, there were six spots. I was sitting in the centre desk, and one of the cool girls looked me up and down and said, 'Hey, can you move down so we can sit together?' Talk about zero foreplay! No social lubricant of, 'Hey, I'm *blah*, you must be new, do you mind moving down?' or, 'Wow, love that you're not crying, can we be friends?' Just, 'Fuck off, you fat loser, cool girls incoming!'

I hurriedly scurried out of the way and quietly cried at the far end of the front row.

Later that day, the two other new girls bumped into me and one of them said, 'Someone told me you were crying earlier in sport, are you okay?!'

I flicked my ponytail and said, 'Oh, what? No, that wasn't me!' Which is a pretty *sweet* recovery.

Every morning after that, I bawled my eyes out over having to catch the bus to my new school. It is the number one reason (and, in fact, also features in reasons two through ninety-nine) for my disdain for public transport as an adult.

• • •

In Year 11, I continued to feel anxious during day-to-day activities. Catching the bus, doing maths tests, getting my period on my school uniform (a light blue dress) and being late, to name just a few—just the thought of any of these was enough to provoke that funny, hot, sick feeling. I got to a point where my quality of life was so low, there was NOTHING that didn't make me sick. I'd feel safe at home, but anything outside of that would cause reckless chaos in my brain.

I was a real music nerd and, like I mentioned earlier, my homeroom teacher Miss Dewar was the head of the music department. This meant music was my safe space at school. There were only four other girls in my year who took classical music, and we got along great. It was always somewhere that I felt confident because I understood everything we talked about. Every weird classical music rule, every transposing exercise, any sight reading challenge—none of it was a problem. Everything that came up made sense to me and I just felt so safe and welcome.

Then, all of a sudden, Miss Dewar took off on leave for an incredible, year-long European holiday. I didn't know if I could cope. I can remember thinking that my safety net had vanished and there would be nowhere safe to hide at school.

Our substitute music teacher, Miss Niehus, was fresh out of uni. I remember us quizzing her on where she'd studied, as if I had the authority to do that, and her politely obliging, answering all of our (probably pretty rude) questions. I was so protective of the space I'd created with the other girls, and so frightened it would be over and done with and it would be another class with an evil teacher.

The four other girls I did music with all did biology too. One day, their class was off on a field trip, and I was taking a double music period on my own. I hadn't really decided if Miss Niehus was someone I liked yet, so I felt very panicked and defensive heading into my lesson.

I remember as clear as day walking into her classroom. She had a massive smile on her face and said hello, and I threw my books and pencil case on the table and mumbled, 'The other girls are all out for a biology excursion today.'

I had my guard up and I was really rude, something I'm not proud of. But by then, the funny, hot, sick feeling I used to only get sometimes was now just permanently in my tummy.

I defended my shitty behaviour in my mind, lying to myself that she deserved it, that she'd just wandered in and taken over.

Miss Niehus kindly said, 'That's okay. I'm sure you can chat with the other girls and go through whatever we learn today when they're back.'

I remember angrily thinking I wouldn't be teaching the other girls anything. I wasn't their teacher, I wasn't getting fucking paid to do this—she was! I didn't have to run anything through with them because they were the ones on a fucking excursion. I wasn't about to donate my time. Get absolutely fucked.

Miss Niehus interrupted my internal anger spiral with a simple, 'How are you today?'

This is a very common greeting here on planet Earth, and most people say it at the very beginning of a conversation. However, at that specific time I'd apparently forgotten this, and got hot and angry again. I felt like she was trying to figure me out. (Gosh, we're all so angsty and important at fifteen aren't we! Gee whizz.)

I said, 'Yeah, I'm fine.' Then she looked at me in a way I'll never forget for my whole life . . . and everything came out. I cried and cried and cried.

Tears that had been sitting in my chest since the mean boys on the bus made fun of me in Year 3, tears that had been sitting in my brain since me not being perfect at something had become a trigger for anger and sickness, tears that had been building for reasons I didn't understand, that had been filtering out slowly in anger and rudeness—they all came.

After what felt like years, my sobbing slowed and I choked out, 'I'm so sorry.'

Miss Niehus rubbed my back and handed me tissues and said, 'You don't need to be sorry. It's okay, but what's going on? I can help.'

The tsunami of misunderstood emotions that followed would be a lot for anyone, but can you imagine some little bitch who'd done nothing to make you feel comfortable at a new job telling you this? You'd make her suffer, surely. But Miss Niehus didn't do that. Instead, she listened as I explained how I'd been feeling incredibly anxious and unhappy and generally just had been living under a grey cloud, and she comforted me and asked whether I'd told my mum.

No.

I couldn't stomach the thought of telling someone who gave me everything under the sun that I felt this way. There was no way I could let my mum know how I was feeling. I was so scared that I would seem ungrateful for my perfect and easy life. What the fuck was wrong with me? I felt so guilty for feeling bad, which fed into this shame spiral of darkness that I was really terrified of, yet also comforted by.

We're talking about a lot of complex emotions here, emotions that many people might not ever understand, experience or believe in—and I was a fifteen-year-old unsure that I'd see sixteen who had just been completely unravelled by a teacher I didn't even like yet.

'I won't tell anyone if you don't want me to, you can trust me. But I think you should talk to your mum if you feel comfortable . . . Or I can reach out to someone, if you need. Tell me how I can help and I'll do whatever I can.'

I caught the bus home after school and when I saw my mum, I popped open like a bottle of champagne at Christmas. I was absolutely off my rocker, and she immediately knew something was wrong. I explained briefly how supportive Miss Niehus had been, and how I had been feeling really anxious and I thought I needed to go to the doctor.

A trip to the doctor revealed moderate to severe anxiety, which I was prepared for, but also major depression, which I was not prepared for. My doctor talked through what that meant and explained some of the treatment options, which included exercise, journalling, eating healthy and seeing a psychotherapist.

I went to the psychotherapist once and got incredibly hot and angry and defensive. I didn't have the language to explain why I felt the way I did, and the person I saw didn't have the right language to ask. It wasn't a safe space for me, so I decided in that split-second that I couldn't go back. I walked out to the car with a fake smile plastered across my face and told my mum I felt WAY better and the psychotherapist was SO great that I didn't think I'd ever have to go back.

I never asked my mum if she knew I was lying to her, or if she knew I was lying to myself, and I literally can't ask her now. But she let it go.

• • •

Looking back and reflecting on this time, I feel really fucking sad. Not just because I'm putting myself back into this very dark period, but also because so many memories of missed opportunities are coming to mind. So many things I said no to because I was just so scared to look silly, or because I was just so far down in the depths of depression that I didn't find joy in anything.

I'm also realising how important teachers are for kids. Mine saved my life.

I've never thrown up in someone's mouth while they were kissing me

I was not very cool at school. There was certainly a time when I was cooler than I had been in the past, but I was never a hottie who boys would hit up on Myspace. I had a boyfriend when I was fourteen, but I didn't have one again until I was like eighteen. Still, there's no way I'm not going to use this book to allow a cool, sexy version of me* to live on in infamy, so here I present the closest thing I have to a crazy hook-up story.

(*Please note: it is not cool or sexy and if my mum was here to read this book, she would tell me to take this out.)

• • •

My best girlfriend at the end of high school was Zoe (real name). Zoe and I were pretty inseparable, but she was tall and thin and had finished with the torture of braces, so her teeth were very straight and lovely, and she was basically MUCH hotter than me. Boys always liked her because she was super fucking smart, but also liked cool music and wore Doc Martens. Whenever we were together, there was no chance a boy would fancy me over Zoe—we've all had that girlfriend who we love, but who really salts our game when we're out on the lookout for hotties. And if you haven't, congratulations, you're the hot one.

I know now that being 'that girl', the kind of girl Zoe very much was, isn't actually only about how you look: it's a state of mind. It took over twenty years of anecdotal evidence to make me realise that some people just *have* it. It's an *energy*. As if at birth, most of us are wrapped up in a normal, plain blanket, while the chosen few get a 'that girl' blanket, which bestows 'that girl energy' (or TGE).

I personally was wrapped in a plain, normal blanket, but that doesn't mean I accepted my 'plain, normal' status. Here's a list of things I've tried over the years to create my own 'that girl energy':

1. Having delicious glowy skin. I do have lovely glowy skin now—having spent a LOT of time and money on it—but it still hasn't given me TGE.

2. Having lovely straight teeth. I thought that because girls with TGE (like Zoe, and one of my best pals, Lain, who looks EXACTLY like Blake Lively) have straight teeth, this must be the thing. If I had lovely straight teeth, I'd have TGE! It didn't work. I now have straight teeth, thanks to a painful year of Invisalign, and yes, the teeth are LOVELY and

definitely make me more confident, but I don't have TGE. I'd hoped that beautiful skin paired with beautiful straight teeth would be a winning combo but still, no dice.

3. Caring about less stuff. Like how Abbi Jacobson or Awkwafina or Lizzo have that 'don't give a fuck' attitude?! While still being high achievers but being so 'whatever' about life?! How do I get that?! Many years of painful and expensive therapy have been personally transformative and I am now a much better person. I have done the fucking work and am now much calmer and more well rounded—but did it give me TGE? Fuck no. Chalk that up to a *loss*.

4. Wearing different clothes. This one is a tough one. I don't have one single aesthetic. For example, I mostly wear plain clothes, but my vibe changes all the time. Sometimes I look a bit more 'femme', or a bit more casual, maybe a bit more 'rock 'n' roll' or whatever, but I generally go for 'effortless chic'—hence the plain clothes. And let me tell you, calling it effortless doesn't mean it is. A TGE outfit on Pinterest does not work on me in real life. MAKE IT MAKE SENSE.

5. Making my own pasta. Anyone who knows me knows that I love Alison Roman. She's a cook who lives in New York and has a zillion online followers due to her laissez-faire attitude and good vibes. She is wholesome and cool and a hundred per cent TGE goals. I thought making my own pasta or bread would give me those same vibes. It did not. It just made me put on weight because I was eating bread and pasta all the time. Why didn't that work for me?

a) Continuing on with Alison Roman's TGE—she always has her nails painted a perfect orangey red. So I started always painting my nails orangey red. This probably was the closest I got to TGE, but still, nothing amazing happened.

6. Jewellery. I thought that if I started wearing cool gold jewellery, it would really finish off my look. But you know how a baby girl is often gifted earrings, a bangle or a necklace? And you look at it and understand the aesthetic but it's not really working? That's what I look like with jewellery.

7. Activewear. Activewear doesn't give me that Steph Claire Smith athleisure TGE vibe, where you just know she did Reformer Pilates this morning and is just grabbing some artisanal bread for her breakfast before running ten kilometres later on. On me, it just looks like I'm going to move house or something. I definitely look like I'm dressing for comfort, not as a fashion choice.

8. Making raw desserts. Two fucking words: Medjool dates. Repeat after me: HAVING MEDJOOL DATES IN YOUR FRIDGE DOES NOT GIVE YOU TGE. Trust me.

So, that's a bit of an insight into just a few of the myriad things I've tried in order to get TGE. It's obviously just not on the cards for me. (But if you have a secret, illegal potion for TGE, please slide into my DMs.)

• • •

Anyway. I'm seventeen, I'm not as hot as my friends, and Zoe has gotten us an invite to a house party with her elusive friends from *another school*.

There's something so cool about having friends at another school, isn't there? It's like you're a celebrity at your own school when you have friends elsewhere. It's the high school equivalent of saying, 'I backpacked around Southeast Asia.' Basic as fuck, but we're all jealous of your worldliness.

Just like when you go overseas and you think you can reinvent yourself, I thought, 'This is my opportunity! I'll be a brand-new Toni and look cool and probably find ten boyfriends.' We weren't far off graduating and this night was going to be a real blow-out. We were excited to go out and do some underage drinking and have fun. My mum had bought me three Corona beers, and I was going to get loose.

First, we got tarted up. I remember perfectly what I was wearing: a tight strapless mini-dress. It was black, it was Roxy, it had little diamantes across the neckline and it was bought specifically for the occasion. My long (bleached blonde) hair was straightened to within an inch of its life, and the front section was teased and pinned up into that little pouf we all used to do. I had black eyeliner all the way around my eyes, and at the time, I had stretched ears as well, to really top off how cool the look was. I was also wearing these killer black heels that Mum and I had bought from Betts.

Mum dropped me off at Zoe's house and Zoe's dad dropped us off at the party. We walked in like the fucking hotties we were, although everyone continued doing what they were doing. We had just found a spot on the back verandah where we could set up for the night when I realised my first party foul: how could I open this beer? I didn't have a bottle opener.

Then it hit me: this is how I find my first boyfriend for the night!

I walked over to a group of boys, who were all drinking beer, and asked in my best hot-girl voice if any of them could help me. One of them could and I immediately imagined our wedding . . . before he turned his back on me and continued talking to his mates.

All good—plenty more where that came from! I had two more beers to open, so could try that sexy 'trick' twice more. My TGE was coming to life!

I was underage and not a good drinker. I didn't know it then but I am a cheap drunk. As an adult woman who knows her limits, I generally only have a cocktail or two these days. I don't really love drinking, and I hate feeling sick the next day.

So those three Corona beers were a LOT for me. I was safe and sound, but silly. I also definitely drank far too quickly to try to look 'cool'. Please don't judge Past Toni; we all make mistakes.

An hour or two into the party, everyone was getting a little silly, Zoe was off having fun and I was making conversation with people, but I definitely hadn't found any of the ten boyfriends. Then a boy walked into the party, and he was so handsome and he had McDonald's. We are going to call him Arthur (fake name). Arthur was super cool—he definitely had male TGE (or what we now refer to as 'BDE', I believe).

The rest of the story is a little hazy, but I'll cut to the part we all came for.

Arthur sits down in the group I'm in.

I think I'm being sexy (???) and that I'm oozing TGE (??!) and I bat my eyelashes at him.

Arthur starts to talk to me.

Arthur is eating McDonald's chips.

I think it's cute to ask for a chip.

Arthur says yes and puts chips in his own mouth.

I grab a chip and eat it.

I realise one chip on a tummy full of beer isn't a good choice.

Arthur continues to smile and puts another chip in his mouth.

I ask for another chip.

Arthur says yes.

I decide that instead of taking a chip from the packet, I'll eat the chip that's already IN HIS MOUTH.

The single chip in the sea of beer in my tummy isn't happy, and . . . I throw up a bit.

Into his mouth.

I throw up into his mouth, everything is on FIRE. NOTHING IS GOOD, AND IT'S THE LEAST HOT THING THAT HAS EVER HAPPENED.

That's just the highlights (lowlights?), but everyone at the party was pretty nice about it, all things considered. Someone made me two-minute noodles to try and make me feel better, and as I was eating them, I remembered my mum was going to pick me up at 10 p.m. and it was like 10.02 p.m.

I sprang out of the seat and ran out to Mum's car, trying to act cool. She took me home and put me into the shower. When I walked out of the bathroom wrapped in a towel, Mum asked, 'How are you feeling, love?'

I said, 'Yeah, way better!' before projectile vomiting the semi-digested two-minute noodles—and one chip—all over her and the floor.

Mum cleaned everything up and then the next day told my whole family. They have only *just* stopped giving me shit for it.

I also never got invited to another one of those parties with Zoe's friends.

You're going to be okay

When I was at uni, as I've mentioned, I had a job in the deli at Coles. I worked with lots of great friends, but it was extremely unglamorous. Other friends had cool jobs where they could sneak their phone in and text their friends while they were working, but we weren't allowed to bring anything into the deli with us. We were dealing with so much food and had so many food safety rules, we weren't allowed to have phones or fake nails or piercings or wear our hair down. Like I said, not glamorous. But so fucking fun. Spraying each other with water, slipping over in that water later on, singing over the PA about what we had on special, and gossiping with my friends. Heaven.

One Saturday, I went to work at 9 a.m., put my phone in my locker, and didn't look at it again until I finished at 5.30 p.m. I grabbed my car keys and phone to see missed calls from my mum. I went to call her back, expecting she needed me to grab something before we closed, and immediately felt guilty because the shop had already shut. As I walked outside to my car, waiting for Mum to pick up, I yelled goodbye to my work girlfriends. On the tenth ring, I was thinking I could just grab whatever she needed from the IGA around the corner, which was always open late.

These thoughts were interrupted when the phone was answered right before it went to message bank. 'Toni, it's Dad. I'm at the hospital with Mum, they think she's had a stroke. I need you to go home and feed the dog. Libby will meet you there and you can drive to the hospital together.'

I stood next to my car, frozen in shock. A million thoughts but also no thoughts streamed through my brain, all at once.

As I realised I needed to remember to breathe, Dad's voice cut through the brain fog. 'Toni, are you there?'

I drove home and fed the dog. My sister pulled into the driveway. Libby and I looked at each other, but I don't remember talking. I guess we did, but I can't remember what we might have said.

We walked into Mum's hospital room together, and saw Dad, our brother, Jamie, and our other sister, Hayley, all standing around Mum, who was sitting up in the hospital bed. I threw myself on top of her and felt her sticky cheek rub onto my sticky cheek, our faces wet with scared tears.

'What's going on? How are you? Do we know what's happening?'

Under normal circumstances, I'm a very intense person. And in a crisis, my intensity only intensifies.

'Mum didn't have a stroke,' Dad said.

Without realising the cadence of sadness in those words, I said, 'Well then, what the fuck are we doing here? Come on, Ma, let's get you home!'

I looked around the room to see everyone tearing up. It was the quietest a room with all six of us in it had ever been.

I locked eyes with my mum, waiting for her to squeeze my hand, just like she had so many times through my life.

When I was scared, her hand was squeezing mine.

When I was happy or excited, her hand was squeezing mine.

When I was sick, when I was anxious, when I was terrified in a movie theatre; when I was heartbroken, when I was depressed . . . her soft hands, squeezing the life back into my little hands.

Then, in that huffy-puffy way you talk while you're crying— as if the words are being strangled out of you—Mum said, 'I didn't have a stroke. I have a brain tumour.'

My world tumbled and crashed and exploded and set on fire and then exploded again.

The rest of the night is a blur. All I remember is having to leave Mum behind in the hospital by herself. I realised in that moment that, all of a sudden, I'd be the one doing the hand-squeezing. I would have to squeeze her hand, because she was the scared one now. She was the one who needed the squeezing.

With tears coming from my eyes and pouring out of my heart, I squeezed her hand and said, 'You're going to be okay.'

I didn't even know this one was a lie.

Things I've picked up along the way that I'll tell you for free

◎ Never leave your favourite jumper at a party. You will never get it back, or find another one that fits as well. I still think about that grey Hurley jumper from 2009.

◎ Drop a pin when you park your car in the city or in a shopping centre you don't know.

◎ An ice cube can get a fresh stain out of ANYTHING. I'm an expert at getting espresso martini off a white linen dress.

◎ The settings on an iron actually do matter, and can melt your favourite cheap clothes AND fuck Mum's good iron.

◎ Still on ironing: if you need to iron something, do it LONG before you need to leave the house. Say, for example, you do melt your favourite cheap clothes and fuck Mum's good iron. You do NOT want that to happen two minutes before you're supposed to be in the car or on the bus.

◎ You have to have a go-to karaoke song. You simply *have* to. Do you know how fucking awkward it is when someone says, 'WHAT DO YOU WANNA SING?' and you go 'uhh . . .'? It's awful. I have three. 'It Must Have Been Love' by Roxette, 'Black Velvet' by Alannah Myles and 'The Best' by Tina Turner.

Also 'Million Reasons' by Lady Gaga, if the mood calls for it, because I love attention and I can belt the fuck out of it. And also 'Something to Talk About' by Bonnie Raitt. Okay, I have five. (Doesn't that sound like the best drag show set?)

◎ Your opinion is allowed to change. I've wasted lots of time worrying that I couldn't change my mind on something I'd had a loud opinion on in the past. My most recent example is changing from silver to rose gold, and now to yellow gold jewellery. But I'm ready for yellow gold and no one can stop me.

◎ Lana Del Rey and a bottle of red wine isn't dinner.

◎ It's perfectly normal for adults to be afraid of the dark. I have no proof but I'm sticking with it. I've chewed through lots of mobile data playing Netflix on my phone at the houses of friends who didn't have hallway lights to turn on.

◎ Never get a manicure right before a rent inspection or moving house.

◎ Again on rent inspections: don't leave it to the last minute. You'll regret it when it's 1 a.m. and you haven't even started cleaning the oven.

◎ Always have tissues in your bag. If you need to do an unexpected poo somewhere—say, you've only just really started drinking coffee and you have one in the morning and then go and do your Christmas shopping and then you realise in Kmart you're going to need to get that coffee out of you

QUICK SMART then, because it's busy, the toilets are fresh out of toilet paper—you're going to need some tissues. And hopefully you can then avoid using the page you ripped out of a notebook and wrote your Christmas shopping list on.

◎ Get a good accountant or someone in your life who loves you and is willing to do your tax return. I am not good with numbers or tax or anything of that nature—but I can cut the music for your wedding! I think accountants—or money people in general—and lawyers are the best people to have in your arsenal. I have the accountant and money people, but if you're a lawyer looking for a friend, please inquire within.

◎ If you're moving house, do not walk around with bare feet, because you'll step on a nail and need a tetanus shot and be rendered basically useless with a dead arm and be no help to your lovely and tall boyfriend (who may or may not be called Taubs) before you move interstate.

◎ Don't pick your nose in the car. People can see everything.

◎ Having the money doesn't mean you need the thing. My mum always used to say, 'The money won't burn a hole in your pocket'—and I need to remind myself of that a lot.

◎ Bleached hair looks sick for approximately three days. If you have hair that grows really fast, like mine, foils are safer. And if you're poor/time-poor/lazy (like me), don't commit. I promise you.

◎ Don't take up a whole new hobby and buy all the stuff before you know you actually like it. Take it from the girl with an entire roller derby kit (did it once) and an entire cake decorating set (didn't do it at all) stuffed into her cupboard.

◎ Always have spare power boards and extension cords in your house. They always go missing or get used and then someone asks, 'Where's that power board?' and someone else says, 'Oh we're using that in the spare room,' and you only realise you don't have a spare when you really fucking need one. I recommend two spares of each.

◎ Don't be impatient to do things you really care about. As an excitable gal, there are many things I have been excited over and ruined for myself because I haven't taken my time. Like surprises I've ruined, or craft projects that I've been so excited about but fucked up because I'm impatient.

◎ When a person offers you something, and you want to take them up on it, do it. Accepting gives to the giver. Think about how awesome you feel when you offer to drive a friend to the airport and they say yes! And think about how awful you feel when they say no and you were only trying to help. Say yes to things if people offer! And if they meant it as an empty gesture and you take them up on it, that's their fault. They'll learn not to make empty offers, so it's a win-win!

◎ Pay the bill the day you get it. This is easy and stupid, but the longer you put it off, the more annoying it is.

◎ Don't bother putting bananas that are almost off into the freezer to make banana bread. Instead of going straight in the bin, they'll just take up room in the freezer for three months before going in the bin. Skip the middleman and don't buy bananas; just buy banana bread.

◎ Don't lend people books that you would like to keep. There is no way of tracking books and you'll forget who has what until years later, when it's far too late to bring it up. My old hairdresser still has my copy of *The Book Thief*. (Pam, if you're reading this, it's actually totally fine. I've since bought another copy of *The Book Thief*. Funnily enough, you're now the book thief. Hope you're well xx.)

◎ Tell the truth. Lying always seems easier, but it never ends up that way. I read this thing the other day that said, 'Our lives are too short to not say what we want in life, in bed and on our pizza.' Seems like pretty good advice to me.

I love change and thrive on the unexpected, part one

I'm a pretty well-adjusted person. When it comes to change, I'm not too bad. After years of therapy and lots of effort and brain-retraining, I have become pretty good at taking on new circumstances. But there were many years when I was not like that, and now, I know why.

• • •

My family were big fans of doing the same thing every year. We found a way that worked and then were like, 'Why fix what's not broken?' and just kept on going with the same thing. And if we were thrust into a different place or experience and it went well, that was added to the list. My mum once won a radio competition on Mix94.5, where you had to call up and answer a question to win a holiday. I don't remember the question, but the answer was *Crocodile Dundee*.

The prize was two nights away at a hotel called Caves House in Margaret River, the wine region of southern Western Australia. So Mum and Dad went down and enjoyed the weekend so much that they went to the same hotel on two more occasions.

While they were there, they went to the Happs Winery and really enjoyed a rosé called Fuchsia, so they bought heaps of bottles that gathered dust in the house, but still more were acquired in bulk on each trip.

They also went to the Margaret River Chocolate Factory and bought all four of us kids a bag of fancy chocolate each, which was SO exciting. I got a bag of cookies and cream chocolate, which is absolutely to die for. And each time they returned from Margaret River, I'd get my bag of cookies and cream chocolate. Because of this, every time I've had the opportunity to get myself some Margaret River Chocolate Factory chocolate, it's always that exact same type. I'm sure the other chocolate they have is fab, but I couldn't tell you! Except for their white, milk and dark chocolate chips, which I can tell you all about.

When you walked through the front door, there were three MASSIVE hessian sacks filled with tiny chocolate chips, and you could 'try' as much as you wanted. I assume this is where Belinda Carlisle was singing about in 'Heaven is a Place on Earth'.

After each visit, my dad said, 'The surf was MASSIVE, Tone, you would have loved it!', until, finally, Mum and Dad took us all down and we stayed at the Prevelly Caravan Park and surfed for a long weekend. And, of course, made a stop by the Happs Winery and the Margaret River Chocolate Factory.

• • •

We went to Broome every year. Every single July school holidays, we would drive 2068.2 kilometres, or 1285.1 miles, or 23 hours and eight minutes, to get to Broome.

Mum and Dad started this tradition with my siblings before I was around, and it didn't stop until I was eighteen. So they drove all that way with three young kids, and then with three young kids and a BABY. There would always be a hanger-on too, like someone's best friend or boyfriend or girlfriend. Sorry, but that's not a fucking holiday for the adults involved, if you ask me.

But it was absolute magic.

Money was pretty tight the first year they went, but Mum and Dad were determined to create some memories, so they begged, borrowed and stole sleeping bags, camping chairs, hand reels for fishing, buckets and spades and fuel for the drive, and the family stayed in a caravan park chalet. They went to the beach and walked along the jetty and did other free things that families enjoy when on holiday, and the kids were allowed to get a Paddle Pop as a treat.

At the time, as I mentioned, things were pretty tight, but Mum and Dad's taste was a bit boujie. On the way to the jetty each day for a walk and a try at fishing, they'd drive past this sign that said Fresh Prawns. Knowing they couldn't afford it, they'd pass it by. Then, on the very last day of the holiday, they said, 'Fuck it!' and Dad drove in there and they ate a kilo of prawns for dinner.

I've been told this story thousands of times, and it always makes me smile.

• • •

When I came along, Mum and Dad were a bit comfier and the holidays to Broome had a major overhaul. They had bought their own camper trailer, so we didn't have to stay in a chalet and we didn't have to borrow camping chairs or sleeping bags.

Dad would spend the weeks before the trip in the shed, getting everything organised. He'd be soldering new lights or new power points so we could charge iPods and phones and whatever else we had to have. When I wasn't helping Dad, I'd be helping Mum go through the kitchen in the camper trailer, seeing what needed replacing and buying snacks and tinned food in case we got stuck somewhere.

There would always be this crazy buzz of excitement between all of us. I haven't experienced a feeling like that since.

For the long drive up, we would get to eat junk food and play Game Boy, read trashy magazines and sing along to Dire Straits for two days straight. The person who was in the very back of the car would be on fridge duty for whenever Dad got hungry, and it was never allowed to be Hayley, because she'd sleep the whole way.

On those travelling days, we were allowed to drink cartons of chocolate milk, and Mum would cut up cubes of cheese and kabana for us to snack on, and these crackers called Cheds that are my dad's favourite. She'd also always cook up a few kilos of honey soy chicken nibbles from the butcher and we'd snack on them cold.

Every road trip I've done since then has included cheese and kabana and Cheds—but I think it's fair enough to skip the cold honey soy chicken nibbles (no offence, Mum).

On the second day of the drive, we'd run out of the pre-packed food. We would stop in at the BP in Port Hedland for fuel, and we were allowed to get those pre-prepared service station sandwiches in the plastic triangle containers. I would get so excited about those triangle sandwiches, as if I'd never eaten before in my life and this was fine dining. I have no idea why. You know the song 'The Teddy Bears Picnic'? I'd sing 'Today's the day the Lodges get their saaaaandwiches!' which is incredibly cute and adorable.

On that second afternoon of the road trip, we'd stop at a service station called Sandfire Roadhouse in Eighty Mile Beach (which is actually 85 miles long), where Dad would fuel up again and we were allowed to get an ice-cream. The main inhabitants of Sandfire Roadhouse, aside from the people, are peacocks. I don't know where they come from or why they're there. Maybe they love beaches that are named the wrong thing? But there are just HEAPS of peacocks.

They'd stalk us around corners and they'd even be in the toilet. It was so creepy, but I guess that's the good thing about doing the EXACT SAME THING every year—you're never surprised by a peacock trying to spook you while you're having a wee.

We'd get to Broome that afternoon, find a spot in the caravan park and set up our site. We had the coolest set-up, and it was so fun creating our little home for the next two weeks. Then, Mum would take us all up to the toilet and shower block so we knew how to get there in the event of a late-night wee in the dark, and Dad would set up the barbecue.

Every year, we'd do the same activities, like visit the Malcolm Douglas Crocodile Park, watch a film at the Sun Pictures outdoor cinema, visit the Courthouse Markets and eat hot cinnamon donuts, have lunch at The Roey, play minigolf at the course outside the caravan park convenience store, get an ice-cream from the ice-creamery, play cards and Balderdash, visit the Broome Gaol and surf every day. Why fix what's not broken? (A lot of very niche Broome-based references in there. Shout out to anyone reading this who knows what I'm talking about, i.e. my siblings and any friends or boyfriends who got dragged along on a Lodge Broome Adventure.)

As I got older, other kids from school would go to the Gold Coast or Bali for their family holidays and I was jealous we weren't going on a plane too—or even going to new places—but I was torn because I absolutely adored our two weeks in Broome every year. Some of my favourite memories are of us up there.

My dad isn't a big fan of flying. I remember asking Mum and Dad if we could go on a family holiday on a plane, like the other kids, and Dad said, 'Toni, if we could drive there, we'd have been everywhere already!'

You could argue that technically, you *could* drive from Perth to the Gold Coast, but it would be awful. You could also argue that there are more places within driving distance from Perth than Broome, but let's not get caught up in the finer details.

The point is that the Lodge family believes in Tradition. The same birthday traditions, same Christmas traditions and same holidays every year. Every. Single. Year.

• • •

Not that we were boring. My mum was a massive fan of travelling and exploring! She loved to get out of the house and she'd take the chance whenever she got it. So much so that another popular family holiday destination was Myuma.

Never heard of it? That's because it was our fucking backyard.

One long weekend, Mum and Dad decided we'd go on a little getaway so, assuming we wouldn't be able to get a booking at Prevelly Caravan Park, we dragged our camper trailer into the backyard and camped out. We weren't allowed into the house except to use the toilet or the shower.

Forgot your Game Boy? Too bad. Didn't remember to grab your book? See ya, book! It was a cutthroat system and it was so great.

This probably sounds quite tragic, but where does the family who hates change go on holiday? *Their literal house.*

My mum really did want to travel and see the world, though. But, like I said, my dad doesn't like to fly. Then one day when I was fourteen, Mum said, 'Fuck it' and booked a trip to Europe for her and me.

• • •

I'd wanted to go to Paris since I was a little girl, growing up obsessed with the TV show, books and movies about Madeline, the gorgeous and brave, tiny-but-mighty orphan from Paris. I'd watch the show whenever it was on ABC Kids and daydream about the old house in Paris that was covered in vines, and imagine being rescued from the Seine by Genevieve the dog. I have gone to Book Week parades dressed in homemade Madeline costumes both as a youngster and an adult.

Fun fact: the sewing machine I have now was purchased the night before a last-minute Book Week parade we'd had when I worked at *Jase & PJ*. I'd handmade a Madeline costume, with darts in the dress and everything. My mum had taught me to sew and when I finished making that costume, I bawled my eyes out at the memories of Mum, and learning to thread a sewing machine, and watching Madeline together on the couch, finishing cross stitch and embroidery kits from Spotlight.

We flew from Perth to Singapore, then on to Heathrow. We spent five days in London, five days in Paris, then five days in Euro Disney, and wrapped up with three days in Singapore.

Mum and I saved up and bought ourselves the fanciest, Frenchest and most chic wool overcoats for our holiday to Europe, even though it wouldn't actually be that cold when we were there. We went in July (don't worry, we went to Broome beforehand!), in perfect time for a pretty gorgeous European summer.

In London, we stayed in this gorgeous hotel in South Kensington and got to walk in the sunshine to the Tube to go and do fun touristy things. The best thing was seeing my favourite musical of all time, *The Phantom of the Opera*, in the West End.

We went for coffee and ice-cream afterwards in a little corner café. It was like something out of a movie. I can still see us sitting there, laughing and talking about how amazing the show was and discussing my dreams of playing Christine Daaé because I would be able to sing AND dance the part—then the camera pans outwards and the credits roll on this amazing movie where a mother and daughter live happily ever after as best friends and nothing can come between them.

With broken hearts, we left London and travelled on the Eurostar to Paris. You know, that underwater train?! Heartbreak quickly turned to excitement about getting to Paris. Finally, after dreaming of baguettes and fromage, we were on our way.

I'm a pretty smart person, but from time to time, we all suffer a doofus moment. Mine was being upset that I couldn't see the fish from the train. I can't tell you how disappointed I was to realise it was a concrete tunnel and wasn't like when you go on the little conveyor belt through an aquarium.

But I took it in my stride and hopped off the train with my suitcase in one hand, my mum's hand in the other and a massive smile on my face. Like weary travellers do, we arrived on the doorstep of the hotel, only to realise it didn't *quite* look like it did on the website. The pictures might have been accurate at one point, but that was probably some years before.

'Muuum, are we sure this is it?' I asked, being the worry wart I am.

Mum reassured me that it would be fine. 'Let's just go in and check it out! I bet our room is great!'

We walked into the reception area, and this older woman simply said, 'Nom?' ('Nom' is French for 'name'. I just googled that for dramatic effect.)

She explained what floor we were staying on and pointed to two coffee tables in a dingy corner of the room to show us that's where our continental breakfast buffet would be each morning. Mum and I shot each other a raised eyebrow, and continued to the lift.

We got stuck in the lift, which was not a great start, and then walked over to a brown door with peeling paint. Mum opened the door, hoping it would be like the Ritz Carlton on the other side.

It wasn't.

It was kind of like what you'd see on an American TV show, when they show the hideout motel of a drug dealer or murderer who's on the run. Two mangy single beds and an old TV with a big back on it, one pillow on one bed and one towel on the other.

Immediately, I started to panic and said we weren't safe, before Mum stepped in to remind me this was an adventure, and said, 'Let's see if we can get some more pillows, hey?'

We pushed the two single beds together, snuggled through the night and lived to tell the tale.

Despite our shock at the reality of the hotel, it actually turned out to be in a great location, and the stress over the continental breakfast was completely unnecessary. With the freshest fruit, flakiest pastries, silkiest butter and creamiest cheese known to man in our tummies, we took on gay Paree!

We spent a few days pretending to be locals in our fancy French coats and eating at McDonald's after visiting the Louvre because the restaurants nearby were all far too expensive. The chic coats made us feel so fancy, even though underneath we were wearing jeans and T-shirts that were probably Billabong or Roxy. But like I said, it was July in Paris—so it was sunny and gorgeous—and we ended up carrying these massive coats for more time than we actually spent wearing them.

On our third morning, we woke up, filled ourselves with pastries and cheese and got ready to see the Eiffel Tower. Of course, we'd seen it from far away, but this day we were going to climb the stairs and go all the way to the tippy-top!

As we were getting ready to go, Mum grabbed her coat. 'Mum I don't think we'll need coats, hey?' I said. 'We've ended up carrying them every day and they're so heavy!'

Mum looked at me, and always being afraid of being unprepared said, 'Tone I don't mind carrying them, I think we should wear them just in case!'

'Nah, fuck that. It's gonna be lovely and sunny, it's fine, we don't need them.'

Cut to the worst weather Paris has seen in 752 years. The Eiffel Tower was shut due to bad weather for the first time in 9000 years—while we were already halfway up!

I've never been so cold in my life. The wind felt like it was actually ripping through our skin, and I wanted to cry.

'Mum I'm so sorry, we should have brought our coats! You were right!' That's just CATNIP to mums, isn't it? *You were right.*

She just laughed and laughed, and we hugged to try and share body heat as we hobbled all the way back down the steps.

This one is one of the most special memories I have. Not only was I lucky enough to go to Europe with Mum when I was fourteen, I was also so proud to watch her take charge, wanting to travel and just doing it.

And until the day she died, no matter where we were going, she'd look at me with a smirk and say, 'Do you reckon we need a coat?'

I just don't have the time

I've always been obsessed with time. When I was a kid, my mum wore a gold Seiko watch with a white face and roman numerals. It was always five or seven minutes fast, and she was *never. Ever. Late.*

It was this point of pride thing for Mum, but somehow, she always got the right balance of being early but never irritatingly early—which is my problem. I'll often stress about being late, and then end up being fifteen minutes early, which is actually too early. Like, you can't knock on someone's door to pick them up fifteen minutes early, because they're still getting ready. You can't rock up to someone's house at 6.45 p.m. for dinner planned for 7 p.m., because if they're anything like Taubs and me, they're still cleaning the toilet or taking boxes from the online deliveries they've received over the course of the week down to the bin.

I do wonder if this is a pattern of lying and self-deprecation, though. Do I just remember my mum being great at everything and assume I'm getting it wrong?

Whenever I recreate a recipe of hers, it never tastes the same. Like, it tastes good, but it's just not the same! I'm never the right amount of early, and my braids are never as tight as the ones she'd do for me. (In my defence, it's pretty hard to braid your own hair.)

· · ·

Growing up in Perth, there were a couple of key events you would look forward to each year. You'd *probably* go to Adventure World sometime during the summer holidays, you'd watch the RAC Christmas pageant on TV (or get to actually go to it, if your parents were brave enough, which mine never were), and you'd hopefully get to go to the Royal Show in the September holidays. I really hope those three things have ignited something in readers from Perth, because for a split-second while writing those down, I got so excited about the Royal Show, I almost went to call my mum.

We went to the Royal Show every single year, and it was the most exciting event in the calendar. When September rolled around, I wouldn't be able to contain my excitement. I've never been the biggest fan of change as an adult, and you're probably about to see why.

About a month before the Royal Show, there would be a Royal Show Guide in *The Sunday Times* newspaper, and I'd scour it. There'd be an in-depth breakdown of every attraction, ride, animal-showing event and performance, plus a map of the showgrounds, and the gold: the showbags. There would be pages and pages featuring every single showbag you could get and listing the pavilions you could find them in. I'd spend that entire Sunday at the dinner table, writing down the showbags I wanted to bring home and how much they cost, before Mum would tell me that was far too much to spend on showbags and I would lie to myself and complain that she was being unreasonable.

I'm actually not taking comments at this time, and maintain that this is a super cute thing to do. Just picture chubby little Toni sitting there in pyjamas with a blue and yellow West Coast Eagles calculator—probably with Milo all over my face—trying to live my best life with zero dollars of my own money, just hoping Mum will bankroll the whole thing.

The September long weekend was a big event for the whole family. Every year, my dad would always go away camping with Jamie, and Mum, my sisters and I would go to the Royal Show. Every. Single. Year.

We'd get ready in the morning, me putting on an outfit I'd organised over a fortnight in advance. Mum would give me my money before we left home, which was normally $20 for extracurriculars, like if I wanted a weird drink or something from the craft pavilions, but did NOT include the budget for scheduled meals or showbags. We'd drive to the McDonald's in Vic Park on Albany Highway and have breakfast. We'd order a

Bacon and Egg McMuffin meal each, mine with orange juice and Mum's with a large cappuccino, and after eating that, we were allowed to get hotcakes! But we always ordered them separately, never at the same time.

Then we'd drive to the Claremont Showgrounds where the Royal Show was held, always listening to Shania Twain or Vanessa Amorosi on the way. We'd park in the carpark closest to the show, always commenting on how it was anywhere between two and five dollars more expensive than the previous year, and we'd walk across to the entrance. The energy would always be electric, and we'd never have to wait in line because Mum would have pre-purchased our family pass at the local independent grocer.

We'd bang a right immediately, heading to the Girl Guides bag-minding tent to store our bag full of jumpers for after the sun went down. Then we'd go to the toilet before we got started on our expedition.

We'd go to the Art Show on the right-hand side, then to the Educational Pavilion on the left (which was always like a 'how flour is made' type of thing), then down to the Animal Farm. Libby would always wait outside because she hated the smell, while we'd look at the ducklings and camels, and I'd hope to get picked out of the crowd of kids to feed a lamb. (I never got picked, not cute enough.) Then we'd all stroll past those shops with funny T-shirts (the ones that say things like 'Take a picture, it'll last longer'), and go into the Fresh Food Pavilion.

By this time, our excitement had churned through the Bacon and Egg McMuffins, orange juice and hotcakes, and the free samples were welcomed. You'd get a tiny plastic shot glass of chocolate milk and a silver patty pan with mushrooms in it, and there was a little stall that did free sausages on a stick too.

Now, I've debated whether to make this book political, but there's something I just can't keep inside. The sausage on a stick used to be free and then, all of a sudden, one year I trotted around the corner to confront the SHOCK that it was now 50 cents! The following year, it would creep up to $1, and then $2. I mean, that's just inflation, isn't it? They're probably $58 each now.

Anyway, we'd continue our walk around the showground, have Red Rooster for lunch and then walk down to Sideshow Alley, where all the rides and games were. The best rides were the fucked ones where someone would always walk away a little greener than they were beforehand. But Mum refused to go on rides, so we'd always play her favourite little game. The one where you drop a coin into the top of the machine and the platform slides in and out and you hope that the coins will waterfall out of the bottom if you put them in the right spot.

This routine was so perfectly timed that by the time the sun was just starting to go down, we'd be back at the Girl Guides tent to pick up our jumpers. Then we'd find something for dinner and settle in to watch the fireworks. On the drive home, my heart would be so full because I'd have had the best day of my life and I'd want to cry because I'd be so excited for next year.

Nah, I'm fine with change, why do you ask?

This one year, I decided to wear a gorgeous pair of black cargo shorts with a blue Hawaiian shirt. Libby and I had stayed up late the night before, watching *Charlie and the Chocolate Factory* on Channel Nine and painting my nails light blue, with dark blue dots forming a flower. Pretty cool. To complete the look, we woke up early so she could crimp my hair, and I asked Mum, 'What time do we get to leave to go to the Royal Show?'

I remember as clear as day her sitting across from us at the dinner table, having her coffee, responding with a massive smile and saying, 'You can get dressed in fifteen minutes.'

I asked, 'How do I know what fifteen minutes is?' and she pointed to her gold Seiko watch, which she wore some variation of for my whole life, showing me how a quarter of the watch is fifteen minutes. She explained how there are 60 minutes in an hour, so fifteen minutes is a quarter of an hour.

'So, it's like a quarter of the clock? So, when you say "quarter to nine", it's fifteen minutes?'

She looked so proud of me.

• • •

I remember my first watch.

Jamie bought it for me for my birthday. It was in a bright yellow box. It was a Rip Curl silver watch with a bright aqua-blue face and Swarovski crystals on the border, surrounding the entire face, that I'm pretty sure I convinced everyone at school were diamonds. I opened it and, before sliding it onto my wrist, checked my mum's watch. I synchronised my own watch to 'Mum Time' and decided I'd never be late either.

At school, wearing a watch was kind of 'my thing'. Everyone knew they could always ask me for the time, and a girl who's name I cannot for the life of me remember once laughed and said, 'Hahaha, we should call you Watch Girl!'

I wonder where she is now.

If you're trying to find your 'thing', I completely advise against time. Always be early, always respect your own time and, more importantly, always respect other people's time. But don't make time your 'thing'. It is less controllable than the elements, but more depressing to count, and devastating to miss out on. It's the only thing where the more you think about it, the more of it you waste.

After my mum died, I just felt like I needed to be early, because she couldn't be anymore. But the obsession with being, if anything, *too* early, means that those moments of worrying I'll be late and lying to myself and making the 'I just don't have the time' excuse have added up to so many hours in my life. So many hours wasted.

So take your fucking watch off and enjoy the time instead of counting it.

But still—always be early.

I've never been broken up with over a fictional character

I've always been a big reader. Which is very exciting because right now, you're reading or listening to a book that I wrote! I was always first in reading group and I would read books faster than Mum could buy them. When I was in primary school, I was in Mrs Elsegood's Year 3 class and Harry Potter was sweeping the Earth. I felt like I was missing out because I must have been the only human who didn't have their hands on a copy of one of the books, but then I got *Harry Potter and the Philosopher's Stone* as a birthday gift.

I fell in love with the universe and the characters. I convinced myself I was a witch and my mum and dad were just waiting for the right time to tell me. It was just like how Harry didn't find out until he was eleven, or how Sabrina the Teenage Witch didn't find out until she was sixteen. Or how Mia doesn't find out she's a royal until she turns fifteen in *The Princess Diaries*. When milestone birthdays would come and go and they still wouldn't tell me I was royal or magic, I assumed it was to allow me one more year of normal life.

But back to Harry Potter. I loved it. I had Harry Potter EVERYTHING. Bedspread, books, board games, the Harry Potter Levitating Challenge, Harry Potter notebooks, pens, Lego, textas: you name it, I fucking had it. I waited in line for every new book outside Dymocks. I'd dress up in costume and Libby would crimp my hair so I could look like Hermione. Libby also worked as a manager at a toy store, so she would always bring home merch and posters for my room.

Having an obsessive personality, it was no real surprise that as I grew up, this tendency towards extreme fandom translated to other series.

Hi, my name is Toni Lodge, and I am a massive Twi-hard. If *Twilight* rehab had been a thing in 2008 and 2009, they would have been the words coming out of my mouth.

I was a bit of a late *Twilight* bloomer. There were a few girls in my year at school who had been reading the books and getting hot for this vampire guy, and there was a real buzz around it because the fourth and final book had just come out. But it just didn't seem like it was for me. I was a Harry Potter gal, through and through, and though I hate to say it, I didn't want to like something just because the other girls were doing it.

Around the same time, I was going out with my high school boyfriend, Josh. Before we get into it, let me just say that Josh is a great guy and we are all good. He has a baby now and is some engineer living this amazing life, so he dodged a bullet and grew up to be a lot smarter than me.

Anyway, Josh and I were super in love. We were together for two years—which is FOREVER at that age—and had a young puppy-love type of vibe, breaking up every five minutes and spending every waking minute smooching each other. It was lovely and sweet . . . UNTIL TRAGEDY STRUCK and I moved to a new school. It was death for our young relationship. We went from thinking we'd be married forever and nothing would or *could* ever split us up, to realising that not seeing each other was actually shit.

We lasted a year at different schools.

But back to the wonders of *Twilight*.

Mum and I were at the shops one day, and *Twilight* was *everywhere*. The first movie was about to come out and the books were all over the place. Merch was going wild and it was all everyone was talking about.

'Have you read this yet, Tone?' Mum asked. 'It seems to be very popular. Let's get it!'

And despite me groaning over it being what we'd now call 'basic', she popped it in her basket and we took it home.

That night, I decided to give it a whack.

I stayed up all night and got halfway through it. I couldn't put it down. It was so sexy and different and sexy and dark and it was just . . . so sexy. I actually couldn't deal with how hot this book was and how much they loved each other and how protective he was of her. You know, all the things a young girl wants. A textbook fairy tale romance!

The next morning, I was almost finished when Mum woke up, and I said 'Mum! This book is so good! Can we *please* go and buy the next three books?'

Mum took me back to the shops, and we bought the next three books. I fucking *devoured them.* I've never read something with such ferocity, as if my life was going to end if I didn't continue reading. It's what I assume heroin feels like, but with more horny vampires.

After devouring these books in a matter of days, I was a girl possessed. I couldn't and wouldn't talk about anything that wasn't *Twilight*-related. And, as it turned out, it was the perfect time to fall in love with *Twilight*, because the movie was about to come out! So as I read the books I could picture what Bella and Edward looked like and it was all very good timing.

Mum and I bought tickets to watch *Twilight* the day it came out—this is how into the series I was. If that isn't cringe enough for you, I'd love to take this opportunity to add that I was super into wearing T-shirts I'd made. It was all born out of wanting to make band T-shirts I couldn't find in Australia (which was most of them) or couldn't afford to buy on Rockabilia (throwback for anyone obsessed with obscure hardcore bands like me, I see you!).

So I went to the cinema with my mum to see the new *Twilight* movie the day it came out, wearing a fan T-shirt that I had made. (Please pause for a moment to let that magnificence sink in.)

It was a plain grey T-shirt from Target (they didn't have white) on which I'd written I LOVE EDWARD with a black Sharpie. If that wasn't bad enough, I'd also bought red fabric paint that I mixed with a little bit of water and splattered it across the T-shirt to look like smatterings of blood.

(Here is where I'd like to offer an opportunity for you to stop reading this right now and move on to the next chapter. That's totally fine. Not only will I allow it, I actively encourage it. Only the brave forge on from here.)

So I wore my homemade *Twilight* shirt. Yes, out in public.

Mum and I watched the movie. I absolutely loved it and fell deeper in love with Edward and also with Robert Pattinson— the lines became murky for fifteen-year-old me. When we got home, I found sheet music for 'Bella's Lullaby' from the film and taught myself how to play it on piano, and downloaded every single song from the movie on LimeWire and listened to 'Supermassive Black Hole' by Muse approximately 12,000 times.

The next day, Josh came over and was, understandably, already pretty freaked out by the fact I had gone full tilt on being in love with this series I'd only discovered five minutes earlier. And that was before he saw what I'd worn to the movie.

He thought my *Twilight* obsession was fucked (fair enough), he left (also fair enough), and we ended up breaking up very soon after, maybe even that day. I remember slamming the gate shut behind him as he left, and, through my tears, saying to myself, 'Whatever. He'll never love me like Edward loves Bella. Who cares!'

This is, unfortunately, not the end of this story.

I was fucking devastated, so the descent into obsession continued. I printed out photos of Edward from the internet, bought every piece of merch I could get my hands on (which wasn't a lot), and even got Mum to colour-print massive A2 versions of photos out for me at work because I had wasted all the ink at home. It was legitimate insanity, but I just couldn't stop.

This was pretty early in Facebook days, and after being used to Myspace, where no one used their legitimate name, I assumed everyone on Facebook was being truthful. My name on Facebook was Toni Lodge (and it still is), so what harm could a cheeky search for Robert Pattinson do?

Shockingly, when I typed his name into the search bar a profile popped up! Now, don't judge me, I was young and in love, so . . . I clicked 'Add friend'. Who wouldn't? THE INTERNET WAS DIFFERENT BACK THEN, OKAY?!

Within a few minutes, my friend request was approved. I couldn't believe it. Robert Pattinson and I were friends on Facebook, here we go! Cue up the Taylor Swift, because it's the beginning of our love story!

Immediately, I messaged him and said something along the lines of, 'Hey, so nice to meet you! Love you in *Twilight* so much lol, how are you?'

And he messaged back straight away and asked me to add him on MSN because it was easier than Facebook while he was on set. We talked on MSN all night. Not even an exaggeration, I heard my mum wake up for the gym at 5 a.m. and I hadn't been to bed.

I dropped every skerrick of information I knew about him from Google into the conversation in as cool a way as I could, casually mentioning music that I'd read he liked, or that I loved the breed of dog he had.

Anyway, feeling on top of the world and like my life was changing, I nervously brought it up with Mum. She was very supportive for someone who knew her daughter was probably being catfished and said, 'Wow, Tone, that's great. Make sure you don't send him our address or anything, okay?'

The rest of the week went past, and I stayed up every night to talk with him (because of the time difference) and word spread like wildfire through my family that Rob and I were talking online. (I called him Rob, obviously, because we were close personal friends.)

Libby came over for dinner one night and was SO fucking sarcastic about it, and I remember feeling very defensive over our relationship. I was so sure that Robert Pattinson was going to fly into Roleystone on his private jet and come to our family Christmas. I pictured him and me going down to IGA to buy bread and having to dodge paparazzi. Genuinely, I thought that's what was coming.

Speaking of Christmas, though, it was early December, so Christmas was around the corner, and Libby was super into burning DVDs at the time. She *acquired* a copy of *Twilight* online and gave me a copy of the DVD for Christmas with a gift tag that said: 'Dear Toni, Merry Christmas, I wish we could be together. Love from Robert Pattinson.'

I was incredibly embarrassed that my whole family knew how tragic I was, but so happy I could now watch *Twilight* as much as I wanted—even though it was a pretty blurry version.

Unfortunately, he turned out to not be Robert Pattinson at all. He turned out to be a girl from America called Rita, who was playing with my emotions from the other side of the world. I realised this random girl, Rita, who had also added me on MSN, was never online at the same time as Robert Pattinson. The lie unravelled and so did I. I still don't think I've fully recovered, and my ego remains bruised.

My mum's dead but it's fine

My mum died very early on the morning of 9 September 2013.

The night before, we had driven to the hospital twice, with the nurses telling us they thought this was it.

Her large, bland hospital rooms were filled with colour and love whenever she was in there. Fake flowers, millions of photos, a canvas covered in multicoloured permanent marker with words of strength from every loved one who entered the room. Everyone knows that hospital smell . . . the pressed linen and weird hot food, the sanitiser and the smells of hope, but also devastation. Every time I set foot in the Hollywood Hospital, I smelled all of that, until I crossed the threshold of my mum's room, where it smelled like Mum.

The smell association in our brain is incredibly powerful. It's like how we can study while smelling eucalyptus and then sniff a eucalyptus-drenched tissue in an exam and the answers will come flooding back, or smell the air before rain and feel like we're falling in love.

Mum's signature scent was J'adore by Dior. Every snuggle, every smooch, every time I hopped into her car after school, every tear-filled breakdown, was accompanied by that perfume. It's something that, when I smell it now, can bring me comfort but also send me to my knees, depending on the day.

• • •

For the final two weeks of my mum's life, even though she was unconscious, she wasn't left alone for even a moment. Someone was always there, making sure she felt loved and that she knew we were there with her.

Even lunches were taken in shifts, and nurses would come and spend time painting my mum's nails so she looked as chic in those final days as she always had.

Everyone had an important role to play, with even Jamie's mother-in-law, Robyn, sleeping on a rollaway bed overnight to keep Mum company, so we could all get some rest.

That final night of her life was the first she had been alone, not just since she got sick, but in her whole life, at least in the years I'd been a part of it. She had spent her time teaching me, looking after all of us, going to work, talking to me about my day while she was in the shower, or taking calls while she was at work, from one of us wanting to find out when she'd be home or to ask if we were allowed to boil the kettle by ourselves to make two-minute noodles during school holidays.

She wasn't able to speak, but she communicated a million words by waiting until we were all out of the room. She didn't want us to see that.

This sounds like a very sad story, and while it obviously *is*, can we all take a moment to appreciate my mum? Sorry, but who on Earth is that selfless that she waits until we're all tucked into our beds having a rest to have a moment to herself before taking off?

Like, it's a sad fucking story, but I like to imagine her waiting to have that quiet moment where there was no noise, just her final smile, her final smell, her final sigh and then that being it.

After all the pain, medicine, needles, operations.

After a life full of laughs, tears, childbirth, full-time work, grocery shopping, yelling, whispers, movies, hand-squeezing, music, traffic, singing, phone calls and kids—it was all over. The one moment of silence she'd been waiting a lifetime for, and it was done.

At the end, is it just quiet and calm? And do we regret asking people to keep it down or to be quiet? Or do we think back on the times it was too noisy and laugh at the insignificance of trying to hear the weather on TV over someone singing in the shower (me) or trying to concentrate on Candy Crush while someone incessantly talks to you about their day (also me)?

There's not a single part of my heart that thinks my mum felt lonely in that moment. I like to think she thought of each of us, and even in that moment of quiet, a quiet she had probably longed for through the noise of life, she filled her brain with the noise of us, one last time.

• • •

We all drive back into the hospital and see her lying there, peaceful and quiet.

We pull all of the colour out of the room one final time and enjoy the last of her love. Enjoy the last time we'll all be in a room together with her, and walk out of the hospital into a world where her scent is in a bottle from Myer for $104, but her smell doesn't exist anymore.

And the noise takes over again.

Reasons the world is against me—people recognise my vagina

No, this is not a cry for help or admission of Kim Kardashian–level notoriety. There isn't a sex tape (lucky you) or minge shots that have fallen into the wrong hands.

When I first moved to Melbourne to join the breakfast radio show *Jase & PJ*, I knew it was the beginning of something great. I didn't know just how great it would actually end up being, but I had a great feeling. Plus, the Lodge Magic was working overtime, so it *had* to be good.

As soon as I joined the team, I hit my stride. I was able to create, joke and laugh all day every day, and even though I had always told people I would be famous one day, I remember thinking to myself, 'This might actually be it!'

A couple of weeks after I started, we were doing a story arc where we tested romantic things that happened in movies to see if they were really possible. Jase was suspended from a rock-climbing wall dressed as Spider-Man, for instance, and recited the lines of the famous kiss scene to his poor wife, Lou, and we filmed it and put it on the internet.

We also wanted to test whether you could run through the airport at the last minute and get to your lover for that perfect kiss that we've all seen so many times.

The team and I were having a chat about how we were going to get this happening and who was going to run through the airport, and I simply said, 'That sounds really fun!' and PJ said, 'You'd be so funny, Tones. Everyone, Toni should do it!' and it was done.

Being a producer for *Jase & PJ*, I hadn't thought I'd ever really get to be on-air or have a shot at the fun stuff. But just putting myself out there in that moment changed so much for me.

The morning we were going to the airport for the stunt, we were fully kitted out. Another producer, David, was going to be waiting at the gate under the codename Romeo, and I was going to run through the airport, including through security, under the codename Juliet, with our video guy, Franco, following me and filming. As you can imagine, that's a real sight to see at an airport. Not only is someone sprinting (it was a light, sweaty jog from me, actually) through the airport like, shocking and something you'd look up from your $18 sandwich for, it's also stressful. Why are they running? Are they late or has something gone wrong?

Romeo and I were both on the phone to the studio, so I was running and holding my phone, and holding a camera, trying not to pass out and also trying to be funny. Not an easy feat, especially for someone not *super* athletically gifted.

The video is very funny (if I do say so myself) and it was the thing that made me realise I NEEDED to make people laugh forever. I'm pretty sure that was one of *Jase & PJ*'s most viewed videos. It was great and so exciting—people started following me on Instagram and saying they loved me and that I was so funny. It was just wild to me that anyone would know who I was or recognise me.

Whenever we went out for dinner or drinks or otherwise with Jase or PJ, someone would always recognise them and it was so lovely, and I remember thinking that would be so cool, to get to meet and say hey to people who love your shit, and wondering if that would ever happen to me.

But after the airport stunt, I started to get recognised out and about sometimes. Not a lot, but every now and then someone would come over and say hi. And this is completely unrelated, but at this point in my life, I had never had a bikini wax. I found this gorgeous woman on Instagram who had an independent salon, and she was very vocal about making an inclusive and safe space for all people to have beauty treatments done, which made me feel super comfortable. I really didn't want some hot-as-fuck nineteen-year-old looking at my nethers and judging my gine.

I was so nervous and I stressed about it nonstop for the whole week in the lead-up to my appointment. But the salon owner was so lovely and talked me through the process and when I told her I was nervous, she chatted with me for a little while to make me feel comfortable. We made small talk for probably fifteen minutes about what I'd been up to during the day, what I did for work, whether I had anything on after this, you know, the usual chit-chat you have before someone is headfirst in your vagina.

'Okay, so, pop off your pants and your undies. There's a little wipe there for you to use, pop that in the bin and then lay down on the bed under the towel, and yell out when you want me to come in.'

I diligently followed her instructions, doing everything she asked, and yelled out for her to come in.

'Great, Toni, okay, thank you. Now, pop your knees up and we can get started.'

Very nervous, but wanting to make her life easier and not be a nightmare client, I did what she said. She smeared the first strip of wax on and, being a professional, continued chatting to keep my mind off the HORROR that was about to occur.

The wax was on and she pressed the strip down, and said, 'Oh my god!' (not something you want to hear when someone has hot wax on your fanny), then, 'I've just realised where I know you from!'

RIPS THE WAX OFF.

'You're Toni from *Jase & PJ*!'

I'll be honest, I wanted to be famous and to get recognised, but I stupidly thought most people would recognise my face, not my vagina.

Things I know my mum would be mad about even though she's dead

◎ Me not getting dressed up to go on a plane.

◎ Me not travelling and exploring when I have the chance.

◎ Me having chipped nail polish.

◎ Me being late.

◎ Me not making time for myself or treating myself.

◎ Me going out and not knowing how I'm going to get home.

◎ White sunglasses (just in general, in any context).

◎ People not putting their shopping trolleys back.

◎ Me not telling people that Mum always had her hair done.

◎ Me not just putting the heater on when I'm cold.

◎ The receipts and plastic water bottles in my car.

◎ The fact we can't waste a whole Saturday together walking around the shops and eating lunch and having coffee anymore.

◎ The fact that Taubs and I didn't put up our Christmas tree last year.

◎ Someone wearing a belt when they've missed a belt loop.

◎ Anyone ever skipping the song 'Jimmy Recard' by Drapht, because it was her favourite song ever.

◎ People not taking their tray back or putting their rubbish in the bin in a shopping centre food court.

◎ That I'm ever sad. She'd hate that.

I never have, and never would, second guess myself

When I was younger, I said I would be famous. I've mentioned this before, but growing up, entering singing competitions in shopping centres, doing singing lessons, piano lessons, guitar lessons, flute lessons, music concerts, theatre auditions and more, was all just preparation for the eventuality of being a famous musician in some capacity.

Every single audition, concert or music lesson, my mum was sitting in the foyer. Or waiting in the carpark. Or cheering me on from the audience.

After a short life filled with art, I wanted to take it to the next level and decided, at around twelve years old, that I wanted to go to WAAPA. WAAPA, for anyone who hasn't heard of it, is the Western Australian Academy of Performing Arts. It's *the* place to go—it's one of the most prestigious arts universities in Australia, and it's in little old Perth.

I went to my first WAAPA open day when I was thirteen, so a fair few years away from actually attending university. I walked into the foyer and was hit with a chorus of people singing and tapping and laughing and playing music. I walked past the dance studios, hearing a piano being played and seeing dancers prance around, then walked past the acting rehearsal spaces, listening to acting students practising monologues and musical theatre students singing tunes I'd sung in the car with Mum for my whole life. My heart swelled and I wanted this to be my life.

My first WAAPA audition was for a ballet course, which I didn't get into. It was exactly like the movie *Center Stage*. Just a million other fantastic dancers who were beautiful performers and hid their nerves far better than I did. I was so nervous beforehand that I yelled at my mum in the car and felt awful about it. Then someone came into the audition late, and when the door swung open, I could see Mum out on the steps. I caught her eye for a split-second and she gave me a massive smile and calmed my nerves.

My second WAAPA audition was for a classical voice course, which I'd decided on after I'd started studying opera and taking classical voice lessons for school. Because I have such a late birthday, I was an intimidated sixteen-year-old in a waiting room with other candidates who were all older than me. Some were seventeen or eighteen, and some were 25-plus: a huge range of life experience and singing experience that only made me feel more nervous. I walked in there and the judges commented on my age, but I sang a gorgeous rendition of 'Pie Jesu' by Gabriel Fauré, and my favourite piece from *The Marriage of Figaro* called 'Voi Che Sapete', and I fucking smashed it. Still, I told Mum it didn't go so well so she wouldn't be disappointed if I didn't get in.

I checked the letterbox with hope every morning for two weeks, then one day found a letter on beautiful thick paper that said something along the lines of, 'Unfortunately, we cannot offer you a place at this stage, but our panel of judges believed your audition showed great promise and encourages you to audition again next year.'

I called my mum, bawling my eyes out, realising the impending doom of finishing high school in one month with no university plans.

• • •

The year after finishing school, I worked at odd jobs and saved no money. The pain of not getting into WAAPA was still too raw to even enjoy playing music or dancing.

One day, I was sitting at my computer, listening to a Pearl Jam vinyl (the song was 'Black'), having a moment with myself and thinking about how great music was. After a full year of telling myself there was no way I could be a musician, I realised that maybe I could make music in a different way—in a way that maybe wasn't as unstable as being a performer.

I got googling and found a course at WAAPA that was exactly what I wanted to do. It was one of the last days I could apply for the intake the following year. I knocked up a portfolio for them, winging the whole thing, and checked my bank account for the application fee of $65. I had $66. Meant to be, right?

My third WAAPA interview was for a sound engineering course. It was on my eighteenth birthday, and my mum sat in the foyer waiting to hear how it went.

I met with the head of sound at WAAPA, Trevor, and he asked about my experience.

'I've never done this before.'

Then he asked about how I made my portfolio.

'I just used GarageBand on my MacBook.'

Then he asked why I wanted to go to WAAPA.

'I've always wanted to be a muso, and now I've decided I'd love to learn all about music production and start my own record label.'

Then he told me I'd mainly be doing radio, film and theatre. 'It's not a rock and roll course,' Trevor said. 'You won't be touching a rock and roll band for years. Plus, this is a very selective course. We only accept ten people a year.'

I met his gruffness with a Toni Lodge Smile™ and told him I was so passionate about sound in general (a lie) that it didn't matter what I was doing, as long as I was in the building.

A week or so later, I got a phone call from Trevor, telling me I'd got in. I was working a shift at General Pants Co. and I listened to the voicemail while eating sushi in a food court. I burst into tears and called my mum immediately, screaming, 'I got into WAAPA!'

As soon as I hung up from Mum (who was also in tears), a girl sitting at the table next to me tapped me on the shoulder and said, 'I know how hard WAAPA is to get into, congratulations!'

I wonder where she is now.

• • •

The night before my first day at WAAPA, I was nervous as fuck and Mum offered to come with me. I wanted to say, 'YES! PLEASE COME! I NEED YOU!' But instead, I said, 'Mum, I think I need to do this on my own.' And I did.

I sat down by myself in a theatre full of other excited kids whose dreams had also all come true just by sitting in that room. I opened the course information pamphlet they'd handed us on our way in and flicked to the sound engineering page. A tall, good-looking boy sitting next to me opened the pamphlet to the same page, and I thought, 'Here's my chance! I'm falling in love at uni!'

'Hi, are you studying sound as well?' I asked nervously.

He said, 'Yeah I am!'

'Oh, cool. I'm Toni!' I said, and offered an outstretched hand.

Taking my hand with a massive smile, he said, 'I'm Ben.'

(You thought that was gonna be how I met Taubs, huh? It was a trick! I wrote it like that on purpose!)

We listened to a long talk, soaking up every moment, and then made our way down to the sound studios to meet the rest of our class and have a chat with Trevor, who gruffly opened my university experience by saying, 'You'll never have a nine-to-five, full-time job in sound. It'll be a life of freelancing and long days.'

As someone who loves security, that hit me like a ton of bricks. I'd never feel settled and I'd never have a full-time job in my chosen field, a field I'd actually chosen to avoid the uncertainty of being a performer.

Immediately, I began to fret over what I'd signed up for, and started feeling a sense of what I now know as imposter syndrome. I was one of only ten people who had been accepted—had I taken away someone else's opportunity, when I'd never even make it as a sound person?

But I pushed through. I moved outside of my comfort zone in that course, made friends and started to learn a lot. I absolutely fucking loved it, but still, that stress of fearing I'd never have a full-time job hung over me.

• • •

After I finished my sound engineering course, I didn't have a job to go to, so I decided I'd keep studying towards becoming an audiologist, and freelance on the side. To qualify as an audiologist, I had one more year to do at WAAPA, and then three years at another uni to become a beautiful little ear doctor. Is this weird and shocking information? I like to think that one day, when I have more time, I'll go back and do my audiology masters.

Well, spoiler! I ended up getting offered a job in radio.

I couldn't believe it—a full-time job, nine to five, where I'd get paid to create audio and make sound every single day! I was so excited, but flooded again with imposter syndrome.

I was told nine-to-five jobs in audio don't exist. Should I have one? Someone else would be far better at this job than me!

Why shouldn't I get this job? Why NOT me?

I'm not experienced at all. I don't even listen to the radio. Hamish and Andy are funny, though, aren't they?!

I can't not do it, can I? How could I pass up this opportunity?

But there are so many better people in audio than me. How am I singled out to have this job? I'm nowhere near good enough.

My brain continued on like that for weeks, well past the day I had actually started the job. After a little while, though, those thoughts slowly faded out, and it turned out I was actually really good at the job! I made great friends and was really enjoying what I was doing. I gained all this confidence and figured nothing could ever bring me down ever again.

Then about a year after I started, the guy who was working in the job above me got a promotion to another radio station, and his role was open. The gig was a natural progression from the job I was in, and all of my audio mentors in radio started to ask when I was going to apply.

I wasn't ready for that! A whole new job to learn, and moving from a position with really close teammates into a relatively isolated role. The other scary part was that I would no longer be part of the creative and advertising team, I'd be part of the content team; the cool and scary people who were on-air and came up with ideas and handed out cans of Coke and cartons of milk on the street.

Feeling incredibly intimidated and not ready, I took the job. Not being confident or equipped with the skills I needed, I got so much support from bosses and mentors. It actually wasn't until then that I realised that no one really knows stuff before they do it. Which is a totally crazy thing to admit, but I had spent all my life looking at people doing things they either loved or were good at—or both—and assuming that this had always been the case!

I watched my mum being a great mum, my friends and siblings excelling in their fields or hobbies, and just assumed I was the only one who didn't have that *thing*.

Turns out, no one really knows what they're doing. There's a lot more room to learn in jobs than I'd ever thought. I mean, it didn't stop the sleepless nights or stress migraines over starting a new job (and didn't make starting new jobs in the future any easier!), but it made it easier to play it cool.

I was asleep

As a musical and arty little queen growing up, I would just soak up any music or creativity or passion for art that was going on around me.

Jamie played guitar and I used to pester him like crazy to play songs I knew so I could sing along with him. My mum was a truly awful singer, just atrocious, and it was one of my very favourite family jokes. She would sing and one of my sisters would yell out, 'GET THE GAFFER TAPE!'

I can remember the first time I ever got her with the, 'Hey, Mum, who sings this? Let's keep it that way!' joke, and the look on her face was just priceless.

It was all in good fun. She loved the attention and the joke, and I think she liked giving us a very fun and harmless common enemy. There was just nothing that made her as happy as when she saw us all laughing or chatting or having fun together and, to be honest, I remember that more than anything else from growing up.

• • •

My favourite thing in the world is waking up in the morning and having a dance in the kitchen while making my coffee. It can turn a bad-looking day into the best one so far—there's just nothing a boogie and some singing can't fix.

It's also why I love to drive. I can sing and carry on as loud as I want, and pump myself up for whatever I'm doing or wherever I'm going. I have lost count of the number of times I've looked over at the lights to see a ute full of tradies laughing at me because I've been giving it my best at car-aoke or steering wheel drumming.

Even though Mum was a SHOCKING singer, I'd allow her the pleasure of singing duets with me, and we'd always give the performance of a lifetime in the car together. Normally singing along to Bonnie Raitt or Shania Twain or Ronan Keating (the ultimate Mum playlist) and laughing at how bad she was. We didn't grow up listening to much music in the house, but I'd always be plugged into my iPod or dancing around my room to the radio, practising singing, playing the piano or practising the flute.

• • •

In 2003, I was nine years old and just obsessed with music. I remember watching Channel Ten and an advert splashing across the TV for a brand-new show called *Australian Idol*.

For anyone who has been in a coma for the past twenty years, *Australian Idol* (based on the American version) was a talent show competition that took you on the life-changing journey of thousands of Australians being whittled down over a few weeks to a top twelve. Then, someone would get eliminated each week to find the winner of a record deal with Sony BMG.

When *Australian Idol* began, a whole new world of showbiz opened up to me. I couldn't believe I'd gone my whole life without this show. It made me even more passionate about singing and I'd hang on to every single skerrick of singing advice and coaching they'd hand out to the contestants and apply it to my own voice.

I was obsessed with one of the contestants, Cosima De Vito, who came third, partly because she was just awesome but also because she was from Perth. I couldn't believe someone from little old Perth could grow up and be a famous singer and move away from home and live the dream I had at the tender age of nine. I also formed my first ever crush on another contestant, Rob Mills. I was a bit weirdly obsessed, to the point where I forced Mum to take me to a charity walk because Millsy was going to be there. This chubby little nine-year-old and her poor mum walked the entire thing, and were rewarded with a meet-and-greet at the end. I got Millsy to sign everything I had on me, and Mum took a photo of him and me together with a Polaroid camera from the 'car accident emergency kit' in the boot of her car. (Back then, people didn't have camera phones, so Mum kept an actual camera in her boot in case she had to take photos of a car accident in an emergency.) I can only assume Mum loved Millsy as much as I did, because of how much chitter-chatter about him she put up with.

In a delightful turn of events, a great friend of mine, Sam, has a podcast called *Confessions of the Idiots*, and he gets different guests on each week. One week, the guests happened to be me and the delightful and charming Rob Mills. Shockingly, he didn't remember our first encounter. It was a very cool full-circle moment and I would have loved to call Mum and tell her about it.

• • •

After *Australian Idol* wrapped up in mid-November, the whole Top 12 were going to go on an arena tour together under the *Australian Idol* banner, no doubt to make extra money and sell merch.

I had to go to that concert. There was nothing that would stop me from going, and maybe meeting Cosima or having Rob Mills fall in love with me. Luckily for me, my birthday is in very late November. I hoped that maybe tickets for the *Australian Idol* concert were on the way.

My mum absolutely loved birthdays. Loved the shit out of them. Loved to celebrate us, and loved seeing us happy and loved giving gifts. A Lodge family birthday was a big date in the calendar. It included waking up earlier than normal to unwrap presents (which Mum stored, wrapped, on the chest freezer in the laundry) before school and work, and then a 'party tea'.

I've come to learn that every family has a different version of birthday dinners, and ours was four courses of party food.

The evening would start with two plastic Tupperware bowls filled with the birthday person's favourite chips. Mine would always be salt and vinegar chips, and either Cheezels or Twisties. These would be enjoyed while standing at the bench or in the kitchen, giving Mum a hand with the cooking. The kitchen would be hot because the oven would be going into overdrive, cooking up the main course.

The main course was a delicate selection of oven party food, like party pies and sausage rolls, mini dim sims, chicken nuggets, puffy dogs (red frankfurts wrapped in puff pastry) and little quiches, all served on the oven trays they had been cooked on. There would also be a cereal bowl filled with little red hot dogs that Mum had cooked in a microwave steam bowl. She always served party tea with those disposable plastic cocktail forks that never actually got thrown out, but were washed and put back on the top of the microwave for the next birthday.

The third course would see the oven trays removed from the dinner table and replaced with two bowls of lollies. The lollies were a mixture of the birthday person's favourites. On my birthday, Mum would buy lolly snakes, Starburst Chews, Sour Skittles and Pascall Caramels, with an Allen's Party Mix thrown in for good measure. She'd pour all of the lollies into a disposable plastic shopping bag and mix them all up, then pour the curated assortment into two bowls and put them on the table. The bowls of lollies were for chatting and eating while Mum tried to find candles for the fourth course.

The fourth course was the pièce de résistance—the birthday cake.

Again, to speak from my own experience and to paint the picture of the best party tea ever, my birthday cake of choice was an ice-cream Freddo Party Cake, but my mum was very partial to a caramel mud cake from The Cheesecake Shop. To be quite honest, I'm not sure any of us really loved the caramel mud cake, but it's what she bought every birthday and no one questioned it.

The house would go dark and she'd walk out from the kitchen with a massive smile on her face, her hands protecting the flames on the candles, and she'd do that thing that everyone does when they're the one to start the singing. That sustained 'Haaaaaaaaaaaaaaaaaa—' until everyone joins in is a scary moment, but thinking about my mum's smile and her prompting the rest of the family to join in makes me so happy. (And we all know her singing was absolute dog shit, so she must have had mad stage fright.)

Everyone would sing and the birthday person would blow out the candles and Mum would take the cake back to the kitchen and cut it up, and the birthday person would get the biggest piece first.

In conclusion, Lodge birthdays = big deal.

Thanks for taking that journey with me.

• • •

This one year in particular, I was turning ten and had my eyes on those *Australian Idol* tickets. I remember this so vividly: my birthday was a Friday and my mum and sisters went late night shopping at Carousel (the 'cool' shopping centre) while I stayed at home with Dad and had fish fingers for dinner and was in bed before they got home. Only I was too excited to sleep, so when Mum and the girls got home, they thought I was asleep but I was actually in my room, wide awake, and heard everything they were saying.

My mum began asking Libby for advice on how to wrap a box because she wanted 'for her to open it and see the tickets'.

THE FUCKING TICKETS! FOR REAL! THEY'RE MINE!

I could not contain my excitement and almost wet the bed! Immediately, images of me in the front row, being plucked out of the crowd by the *Australian Idol* Top 12 and singing with them filled my nine-year-old mind. I realised I'd have to think of something cool to wear.

All of the excitement that I was experiencing alone in my room was what my mum had hoped to see on that fateful Friday morning of my tenth birthday. Unfortunately, she would see no such thing.

The next morning, I leaped out of bed and couldn't wait to have my toast and Milo and open my birthday presents. My mum gave me a massive snuggle and we sat down. I worked my way through the mountain of awesome presents, like new clothes and books, and then it all came down to one wrapped box.

Thinking back, ten-year-old me can feel the excitement radiating off Mum, and I know exactly what's coming. I open the box and see the tickets, and immediately look at the seat numbers. I notice they're row D. As fast as I see the tickets, the excitement and images of being plucked out of the audience from the front row vanish.

I say, 'Oh . . . they're really far back.'

Can I VERY VERY quickly just acknowledge that I know I sound like a little bitch, and I'm really embarrassed at how I reacted. I am not a good liar, and I just focused on something so incredibly unimportant because all of the excitement had already been expelled from my brain the night before, when I overheard that I was getting the tickets.

My mum was really upset that I didn't seem excited. Libby lit me up in the bathroom because I was such a little brat. 'Didn't you know that after A, B, C, D, it goes AA, BB, CC, DD, you're in row D! You are right at the front! Mum spent hours on the phone trying to get those tickets! Why are you so ungrateful?'

I was really embarrassed and felt AWFUL for hurting my mum's feelings, so I went up to her room, where she was getting ready, and apologised for not seeming grateful. I was just really overwhelmed and didn't know what else to say.

I could tell she'd been crying, and it broke my heart. I did my best to reignite my excitement and she started to feel happy because of how excited I was, but I didn't have the heart to tell her I'd heard her talking about the tickets, so I didn't.

She still put on my party tea that night.

When the concert rolled around, I wore a white Billabong T-shirt, white wide-legged, three-quarter-length Billabong board shorts and brand-new white Nike runners. I had my hair slicked back and Libby made me a bright green sign that said COSIMA ROCKS.

We were really fucking close to the front, actually. It was awesome. I absolutely loved it and everyone at school thought I was super cool for going to a concert with my awesome mum.

Unfortunately, despite being so close, I didn't get picked out of the crowd.

• • •

About a year before my mum got sick, I bought her one of those books you buy for your mum where it has prompts and you fill it in by writing your favourite things about them and your favourite memories. One of the prompts was 'I'm sorry I lied when . . .' and I completed the prompt, finally telling her that I wasn't asleep and I'd overheard her talking about the tickets and I was so, so sorry.

She forgave me and it felt so good to finally have her know, but I still feel so guilty over it to this day. I'm really embarrassed that everyone knows I acted like a little brat, and also that I was obsessed with *Australian Idol*.

(Please don't tell anyone.)

I don't need therapy, part two

When I was 21, Taubs asked me to move in with him. So I moved house for the first time in my whole life, out of my childhood home and into a new home with Taubs and one of his best mates, Adam. My mum had died a year and a bit earlier, and I was so excited for a new chapter of life.

We'd found a brand-new unit in Bayswater right near the train station and my eyebrow place. Chic! They'd barely put the door handle on when we moved in, that's how new it was! It had cream-coloured tiled floors and freshly painted white walls, and we talked about how there was definitely enough room out the back for an inflatable pool and how there would be so many amazing party nights there. Being so excited about this great new life, I just felt invincible. Playing house with my handsome boyfriend, living with a mate, eating whatever we wanted. It felt so cool and new.

I was still studying at uni and working at Coles to support my cool new life. One afternoon in the deli, I got these insane shooting pains in my chest. Most of the girls I worked with happened to be studying nursing and, like any normal person should, they all panicked immediately. I lied and assured them there was absolutely nothing wrong, and I must have lifted a box of frozen fish using my back instead of my legs.

My brain had decided it wanted to ignore all signs of this being something serious, and I let it. Not because I wasn't freaked out, but because I was. I was really scared—so scared that I didn't want to deal with it at all. Kind of like when you drop something in the bathroom and it smashes everywhere and you just want to close the door and walk away. Since my mum had died, I was freaked out about *everything*. Her dying had just made me think that every single thing I did was going to lead to me dying, or that other people I loved could drop dead at any given time.

The complexity of grief is something I am wildly unqualified to speak about at the length I do. But while I am not a doctor and merely a potato with arms, legs and a heart, I know there is nothing you can do but wade through that deep water and ride the wave. No two experiences of grief are the same, and that's really hard to acknowledge too.

At this point in my life, my grief decided to control how I would handle certain situations. And the crazy thing about that is that not only am I not a doctor, neither is my grief! So

I definitely shouldn't have let my emotions run point on this experience.

The chest pains came again later that day, then three or so more days went by and their intensity grew. It felt how I imagine it feels to be shot. I was in so much pain that I couldn't walk from the kitchen to the couch without getting puffed. I finally decided the best thing to do was to go to the family GP (surely the HOSPITAL would have been a better choice there, but okay). After having a quick look over me and listening to my symptoms, my doctor sent me for every (expensive) test under the sun, under the instruction that if I experienced any shortness of breath, I was to go to the nearest emergency room straight away.

There is NOTHING that makes you more aware of how shallow your breaths are than knowing that if they get shallow, you have to go to the emergency room. Just thinking about needing to go to the emergency room kind of makes your breath shallow, and the breath getting shallow makes the breath *really* shallow, so you can imagine the overthinking that would follow that conversation.

The first thing I did was a regular ECG with the nurse who worked in the GP's clinic.

For anyone who doesn't know, an ECG, or electrocardio-gram, records the electrical signals in your heart. It's a painless test used to quickly detect heart problems (yes, I just googled that!) and it's fairly common. They stick six sticky little pads on you and hook you up to a machine that tells the future (or something).

Unprepared to be seen topless on this particular day, the funny, hot, sick feeling came and warned me danger was ahead. Over the years, I had given my brain so much power that it decided when and where it got to be in charge, and there was nothing I could do to overrule it. Panic set in and my chest tightened. The pain returned with a burning anger that made standing tiring and my head dizzy.

The nurse handed me a gown and asked me to get undressed and pop on the gown with the opening at the front, so she could stick the pads on me. I calmed myself down, undressed, did the test and the nurse said, 'Everything seems pretty normal!'

I wanted to scream. Nothing *felt* normal. It was like a tree had fallen over and was crushing down onto my chest every time I walked or took a breath or spoke—but if it 'seems pretty normal', let's just ignore it!

This seems like a good time to add that I was regressing into old habits of anger and defensiveness. At fifteen, these habits were understandable, because I didn't know how to communicate or what was going on, but at 21? Completely unacceptable.

I also just didn't want to be that person! I love smiling and making other people laugh and having fun, and I didn't want to be this person who became angry and defensive and fucked-off for no reason.

I got cranky and snippy, left the doctors and booked in for test number two, which was another ECG, but with a twist.

And when I see something explained as having 'a twist', I get so angry because it's incredibly unoriginal and lazy—but thanks for buying my book anyway! (If you've stolen this book off the internet, then I will be angry AND disappointed.)

People often don't believe me when I tell them this story, but the 'twist' in this tale is that I had to have this ECG while running on a treadmill. RUNNING. ON. A. TREADMILL.

If you cast your mind back to the part above, when I explained the process of an ECG, you'll remember that you have to undress and wear a hospital gown with the opening to the front during the test to stick the pads on you, and this one was no exception. So not only am I running on a treadmill, but I'm also (basically) naked. I'm (basically) naked, and I'm running on a treadmill.

Let me paint you a word picture: a short, chubby 21-year-old girl with no prior fitness experience going from a walk to a slow jog and then building up to a run on a treadmill, wearing just underwear and a paper hospital gown worn the way one would wear a trench coat. From the paper trench coat trails thousands of wires (probably ten wires) checking my vitals.

I'm going to let that image soak into your brain for just a moment.

Remember earlier when I described childhood swimming lessons as torture? I TAKE IT BACK. I'd take another eight billion years of that over the half-hour of running (basically) naked on a treadmill in front of medical professionals.

As a chubby person, it's always very interesting seeing a medical professional, because you know that no matter what you're going in to talk to them about, they will bring your weight into it. 'Oh, you have depression. Have you considered losing weight?' 'Psoriasis? Is it because of your weight?' 'Ingrown toenail? It must be the excessive weight you're carrying around on those little hooves!' The last one hasn't happened to me, but this is actually my book and I'm allowed to use artistic licence for both comedic and illustrative purposes.

I was already incredibly scared of having all of these health professionals explain that my chest pains were being caused by visceral fat around my organs and the only option was for me to receive a pig heart (I don't know if that's a thing?)—but I was also on full display, and they were just watching my heart rate on the monitor get higher and higher as I walked, and hearing the creak of the treadmill every time I took a step.

Let me tell you, this process is not good for someone with:

a) a potentially bad heart;

b) mental health issues;

c) body image issues; or

d) a dead mum (doesn't help anything, in my experience).

I lived through the embarrassment of the century, put my clothes back on and paid $300 for the privilege.

• • •

Test number three was an echocardiogram. An echocardiogram tests the action of the heart using ultrasound waves to produce a visual display for the diagnosis or monitoring of heart disease (yes, I googled that one as well) and is basically painless.

Given that, at this point, I felt like a pin cushion from all the blood tests, I found myself actually kind of looking forward to something that didn't physically hurt. This was, of course, before I found out about the embarrassment and emotional scarring.

You actually might be shocked to learn this, but I don't embarrass very easily. I am an anxious little pigeon, but it takes a lot to really embarrass me. My philosophy is that if I fall over, I'd rather burst out laughing so that other people around me know it's okay to laugh, because I'm sure it was very funny to watch me topple over in the middle of a busy street or walking up the escalator at the airport—both of which have happened to me. I would rather give people a little giggle than have them pity me because I've fallen over on the bus when it has suddenly stopped in traffic, or sprayed perfume directly into my eyes in a department store. (Yep, both of those happened too.) I take most things in my stride or turn them into jokes. Some people don't like this. The doctor who was performing my echocardiogram was one of those people.

The doctor called me in and I politely said hello and asked him how his day had been. He ignored my pleasantries, responding with instructions to undress from the waist up, put the paper hospital gown on with the opening at the front and wait on the bed.

He returned a few moments later and knocked on the door; I was smiling nervously while sitting on the bed. Let's not forget that at this stage, I've been naked a lot, AND run naked on a treadmill. By this point, I've been seen naked by fewer people in a sexual way than I have by doctors, and it doesn't get any less weird.

I was uncomfortable because my body was exposed, and I was nervous because I didn't know what was wrong and I was stressed that my mum wasn't there to look after me or hold my hand, and I was panicked because I was paying for all these tests and I'd just moved out of home and I only worked at Coles part time, which I couldn't even do at the time because I wasn't fit for work.

That's a lot of traffic for a tiny brain trapped in a naked, chubby woman's body while she is exposed in a doctor's office.

The doctor asked me to lie down on my side with my arm above my head and under my ear. In the tense discomfort and awkwardness that was sucking the air out of the room, I decided to add some commentary. 'Oh, a bit like Rose in *Titanic!*'

Very smooth, Toni.

I lied to myself that he'd never heard that one before.

I was lying on my side and my boobs flopped down in awkward triangles and found a spot on the bed, one on top of the other. I was exposed and in a very unflattering position, especially where the breasts were concerned.

The doctor, unimpressed or simply uninterested in my commentary, said, 'I'll need you to hold your right breast up out of the way, and I'll put pressure here on your chest.'

I made a scooping gesture with my hand and giggled as I hooked my breast out of the way. 'Now just stay as still as possible,' he said sternly.

Before I get to the next part let me put it out there: I respect all jobs. I know all jobs take skill and concentration, especially in the medical field where you have to be on your game and take what people say very seriously. But when I've got my tits out, surely you can meet me halfway with a smile or an anecdote to cut through the tension?

After instructing me to stay as still as possible, the doctor pressed the ultrasound thingy covered in jelly really firmly into my chest. The image of my heart came up on the screen.

When you picture an ultrasound, you imagine the Hollywood version of a beautiful, glowing person with a smile and perfect teeth hearing their baby's heartbeat for the first time. As my doctor moved the ultrasound thingy around, my head filled with images of a pregnancy ultrasound, and I nervously laughed and said, 'Oh wow, you'll have to tell me whether I'm having a boy or a girl!'

Without missing a beat, straight-faced, he said, 'I'm going to need you to stay as still as possible.' Feeling scared, and embarrassed that my joke didn't land, I lay as still as I could.

After what felt like an eternity, he finished the test and I scraped the ultrasound jelly off my body and got dressed. I paid my $400 and decided it would be best to work on my comedy elsewhere.

• • •

The final part of this horrifically unfunny journey was seeing a cardiologist. He was the most warm and comforting person I had seen, and I was so relieved that the person who was about to tell me I'd only live to 23 had some bedside manner.

'You are the healthiest person I've seen this year!' (Please bear in mind it was only March.) 'I've reviewed every single test we've put you through, and you're perfectly healthy. Can you describe the chest pains to me?'

I described them the same way I had to every other doctor who'd asked. After pondering, he asked, 'Have you had any large life events or traumatic things happen to you recently?'

Which I thought on for a moment, and then said, 'Well . . . my mum died about a year and a half ago.'

The very fancy cardiologist leaned across his desk and tenderly said, 'Miss Lodge . . . we can detect many ailments of the heart with these tests, but heartbreak can't be detected, and that's what you're suffering from, I'm afraid.'

I'm sure we continued talking. I'm sure I paid the bill, and I'm sure I walked back to pay for parking, and I'm sure I wandered around looking for my car in the maze of the hospital carpark, but all I remember is sitting in it and bawling my eyes out.

I've said it before and I'll say it again: the complexity of grief isn't something I'm an expert at speaking about, but I'm an expert at feeling it. And boy, did it hit me like a ton of bricks right then, in my Toyota Yaris, surrounded by empty, discarded plastic water bottles.

I regurgitated this information to my family GP at my next appointment, who assured me that's what he'd thought it was all along.

Grief.

Grief, *physically manifesting in my chest.*

A long year of holding in my sadness, my tears, my feelings and my love for my mum.

• • •

What happens to all your love for a person when their body is gone? Where do the memories go? What does your brain do with the phone numbers you've remembered for your whole life? Or the lyrics to the songs we used to sing together in the car? Does all of that just sink to the bottom of your brain-drawer, like your least favourite T-shirt or the knickers that give you a day-long wedgie but you refuse to throw out?

My mum isn't an old pair of knickers. I don't want that to happen to her! I want her to stay at the top of my brain and the top of my drawer, like my favourite knickers.

Someone who is comparing their mum to knickers needs help. I'd be lying to myself if I said that wasn't true. But as the title of this book suggests, *I don't need therapy.*

Things I had to do after my mum died that I didn't think would break my heart

◎ Buy my own shampoo and conditioner.

◎ Delete her number from my phone.

◎ Tell people I bumped into after not speaking for a long time when they asked, 'How's your mum?' that she'd died.

◎ Find someone else to do my eyebrows.

◎ Go to the theatre and watch musicals with people other than her.

◎ Set up my own health insurance.

◎ Experience Mother's Day without a mother to spoil.

◎ Realise we'd never have new photos together.

◎ Sing alone in the car.

◎ Call no one instead of her.

◎ (Finally) throw out the last pair of socks and knickers that she bought for me.

◎ Pick a dress to wear to her funeral.

◎ Not call her on her birthday.

◎ Hear songs she loved.

◎ Do things and take risks without her cheering me on.

◎ Laugh.

I'm good, thanks!

After a long early morning turned into the sun rising for another day to begin—a day where people could snooze their alarm instead of going to the gym, or wake up and make a smoothie and live better than the rest of us—I was lying in bed watching *The Mindy Project* and feeling heavy with emotion. It was as though I was falling in and out of consciousness. I was fully aware of what was happening on-screen, but my inner monologue was turned up to eleven.

My mum just died.

I feel relieved she's not in pain anymore, but I feel sad because my mum just died. But she's safe and free now, but I'm stuck here. Why did she do that? Why did she leave me? She's supposed to be the only person in the world who I can trust to never abandon me and now she's fucking gone! Haha, I love this episode. Why am I laughing? Am I allowed to laugh? EVER AGAIN? How do I make lasagne? Why didn't I take the chance to learn that from her while she was here? So much wasted time! But finally, she's safe somewhere, wherever she is . . .

Where is she? Am I religious now?

These hyperactive, incessant thoughts were interrupted by hearing the TV and the kettle switch on outside my bedroom. People were waking up and my dad was making a cup of tea and putting the news on.

Are we really watching the news? Is that normal? Is me walking out into the kitchen and having some toast or having a shower allowed? Are we supposed to never eat or consume information or shower or do our skincare again?

Or is it normal to keep on going? Is it too soon to keep going? Are we supposed to stop too?

I decided toast and the news felt normal, and we started our morning with regular idle chit-chat and ignored the elephant in the room: the fact that we needed to make arrangements and plan my mum's funeral.

• • •

We went to plan the funeral, and said lovely things like, 'Those flowers are gorgeous!' and, 'Oh, Mum would love that,' even though, on the inside, it felt like the fabric of the universe had been torn into a million pieces. Millions and millions of tiny pieces of my soul were floating around, and I was talking about how lovely flowers could be.

The funny thing about planning a funeral is that every single person is feeling like that while also being polite to the lady facilitating the chat.

'Hello, how are you?' I mean for fuck's sake, what do you reckon, darl?

But we responded with, 'I'm good, thanks! How lovely is the weather today?'

Grief is just so fucked.

We picked the nicest flowers for the occasion (???) and headed home to . . . organise? Clean? Drink? Eat? Who knows what to do. I hope one day someone writes a book of things to do after planning a funeral.

But we went home and picked songs for the service and I edited a bunch of music so we had long versions of everything and didn't hear the music loop. It's a funeral—no one needs that. It's fucking depressing enough.

The next day was filled with a Lodge family working bee. Some family friends came and lent their time and hands to clean the house for the party wake. We had people dropping off food and swinging past with flowers and saying nice things like, 'I'm so sorry about your mum.'

Saying sorry about death is, in my humble opinion, just the worst fucking thing you can say. You're not sorry. You didn't kill her, you didn't do anything, so why should you be sorry? Say it like it is. Tell me you're sorry for how I must be feeling, but acknowledge her being dead is shit. Because IT IS SHIT. It's awful.

I was in a cesspool of emotion, worrying if I'd ever recover, but also fussing over flowers and trying to find the time to call people who needed to know that Mum's funeral was that week and then also politely responding to someone saying, 'I'm so sorry,' with something along the lines of, 'Thank you, that's okay!'

It wasn't okay. I needed to get my fucking eyebrows done, and did I need to bring a date? To my mum's funeral? I'd probably want someone to hold my hand. Should I bring a boy? Imagine that incredibly honest phone call.

'Hey, it's Toni!'

'Hey Toni! How are you?'

'I'm good, thanks! Hey, listen, I have this thing on tomorrow, if you wanna come?'

'Oh yeah, what's on?'

'My mum's died.'

'Oh wow, I'm so sorry about your mum.'

'Aw, thank you, that's okay! So anyway, her funeral's tomorrow. I think I'm going to be feeling really emotionally vulnerable and would love to have someone there to drunkenly make out with afterwards when I've had too many wines.'

'Oh . . . sorry, I have something on tomorrow.'

'Oh okay, no worries, all good! See you soon!'

Funnily enough, I actually did text a boy after my mum's funeral while drunk on emotions and finger food, and he was out doing something (or so he said) and was a real gentleman about it and never brought it up again or made me feel embarrassed for BOOTY CALLING HIM AFTER MY MUM'S FUNERAL. (Sorry, Ian.)

Like I said, grief is so fucked.

• • •

The day before my mum's funeral I realised I didn't have anything to wear that wasn't built for grinding on some dude in a nightclub or seeing a band. Incredibly, the 'Mum's funeral' part of my wardrobe was fresh out of outfits. So, Libby, Hayley, my sister-in-law, Chelsea, and I tackled the problem. Fresh from planning a funeral and cleaning the house, we headed to the shopping centre to look for something for me to wear.

Just like my wardrobe was fresh out of 'Mum's funeral' outfits, Myer didn't have a section for that either. We walked through a few shops and everything was just not very *me*. I was only nineteen years old and I barely had a sense of style yet, which made it particularly tricky to find an outfit while my brain was split in two.

We walked down to one of those young people shops, where the music is loud and the clothes haven't been steamed before they're put out on the floor, so you have to do it when you get home. Everyone working there was a young woman, each one of them more gorgeous than the next. They wouldn't find it difficult to get dates for their mums' funerals.

We walked into a reception of smiles and 'Hi, how are you?!' Before I had a chance to reply with 'I'm good, thanks!', I was interrupted with the spiel of 'We have a sale on today, if you buy 65 pieces of clothing you can buy a tote bag for $2!' or whatever they say.

I grabbed three dresses off different racks and my shopping supporters waited patiently outside my fitting room for the fashion show. I slid the curtain across and prayed to fucking God that the dresses fit, because a breakdown about not liking my body was not going to help me get this done any faster.

I slipped on the first dress. It fit, it looked okay, but it wasn't quite right. I walked outside and my sisters read my face and said, 'That looks okay . . . but it's not quite right, is it?' I shook my head, and the girl in charge of the changing rooms, who was holding discarded clothes, walked over, BEAMING, and said, 'Oh my God, babe, love that one!'

I mumbled out a small 'thank you' and jumped back into the changing room.

The second dress didn't fit—and of course it was my favourite of the three. Babe Girl banged on the wall next to me and asked if I need any more sizes or any help zipping up, to which I replied, 'No thanks, all good!'

By this point, I'm getting a bit tense and overwhelmed. Mostly because the dress doesn't fit, but also because I've got people with me to go and get me another size, should I need it, so please just stop banging on my wall and calling me 'babe'.

And the dress didn't fit.

And my mum is fucking dead.

I knew it wasn't Babe Girl's fault, but I was starting to get a bit hot. I abandoned ship and tried on the third dress. It fit me perfectly and actually looked really nice. Conservative and 'funeral-ly', but still me. I walked out of the change room and my sisters all smiled sweetly and told me how nice I looked.

Babe Girl walked over again, still holding the mass of discarded clothes and said, 'Babe! That is THE. ONE. Love that!'

I mumbled out another 'thank you', all the while getting hotter and more uncomfortable with the conversation, and I attempted to smile at this girl who I was trying to convince myself wasn't mean.

She followed up by saying, 'Like, honestly, I've seen so many girls try that one on and you look gorgeous in it! And so versatile too, you'll get so much wear out of that one! What's the occasion?'

I was standing in the middle of a shop with music pumping overhead in a dress I hadn't purchased yet with no shoes on. Everything slowed down, like a replay during a sports match on TV. I was so overwhelmed that I couldn't even do Babe Girl a favour and lie.

'It's for my mum's funeral tomorrow.'

The girl's face dropped. She clocked my sisters' glum faces then looked back at me. She straightened up, threw the discarded clothes over her shoulder and said, 'I'll just leave you guys to it, shall I?!'

I bought the dress, and wore it to my mum's funeral.

• • •

A few years later, I lived in a share house and was away for the weekend. My housemates had a party and a girlfriend of mine from work went through my closet to find something to wear out to the club afterwards. Digging into the depths of my closet, she chose the dress I wore to Mum's funeral.

It was a really weird feeling. My mum would be happy it was getting worn again, but I couldn't believe the dress was out on a body that wasn't mine, being worn for reasons other than those intended. Maybe the dress enjoyed being taken out for a night on the town.

But Babe Girl was right—it was so versatile!

Things that are my personal equivalent to the first bite of a Double Quarter Pounder

◎ Fresh flowers. I always promise myself that if I ever win the lotto, I'll get a fresh bouquet of flowers delivered to myself and my friends each fortnight. Nothing makes me happier than fresh flowers in the house. It makes it look like I have my shit together and makes our house seem fun and colourful.

◎ Remembering when my mum dropped precious goods in the driveway. My sister Libby is a really good baker. Loves to cook, loves to bake and loves to feed people she loves. One night, Mum and I went to Libby's house for dinner and she made a massive, veggie-filled pumpkin soup and homemade custard tart, one of Mum's and my favourite desserts. We finished the whole thing off and grieved the end of a delicious dessert, only for Libby to present us with a second custard tart to take home and enjoy over the weekend. We drove carefully the whole way home and when we got back, Mum took the precious cargo out of my hands, not trusting me not to drop it on the way inside. But then she fumbled over her car keys and dropped the custard tart in the driveway, and we both peed our pants laughing. I'm pretty sure I rang Libby and told her that Mum hated the tart and threw it on the ground—#JustSisterThings. It makes me smile whenever I think of it.

◎ When Taubs and I first started really getting to know each other, and I was trying very hard to impress him. We were texting one day about our favourite movies, and there were so many I hadn't seen that he said he'd show me next time we were together. This is pre-Netflix and Chill days, by the way. Watching movies back then meant bringing DVDs or a hard drive full of video files that had been 'acquired'. Taubs mentioned he wanted me to watch the movie *Spirited Away*, the Studio Ghibli film. I said I'd seen that and hadn't really liked it, to which he expressed surprise and seemed upset. I told him, 'I'm just not that into horse films?' and he laughed so hard, realising that I'd thought he'd meant *Spirit: Stallion of the Cimarron*, where the horse is voiced by Matt Damon. Whenever I say I don't like a movie now, Taubs says, 'Yeah, you're just not that into horse films, and that's okay.'

◎ One night when Taubs and I were partying with our best pals, Jag and Lain. I worked with Jag at *Jase & PJ* (you might know him as Producer Alex) and he, his now wife, Lain, Taubs and I were basically inseparable. We'd had a long night drinking espresso martinis and dancing in the lounge room. Taubs and Lain were sitting on the couch, chatting away, and Jag and I commanded their attention, wanting to show them our dancing. Jag grabbed me by the waist and dipped me down before twirling me and then grabbed my arms and held them behind my back, causing my button-down top to pop COMPLETELY open. On this night, I happened to not be wearing a bra, so my naked boobs flopped around for everyone to see. It was the funniest thing ever, and every week, in our group chat, someone will say, 'Remember when Toni's boobs popped out that night?' and it makes me smile like nothing else.

◎ Reading a book in the sun. There's just nothing like a book getting warm in your hands.

◎ Little things, like Taubs bringing home treats or reading my mind. He never, ever forgets things I mention I'd like to try or that I like. He also has this habit of reading my mind. Just the other day, I was thinking about this Japanese chilli pepper (Nanami Togarashi) that I wanted to get, and that afternoon he came home with it and said, 'I saw this at the shops and thought of you instantly.' It's something that reminds me of my mum a lot—she was a great mind-reader too.

◎ When people say they love the *Toni and Ryan* podcast. Knowing that people listen to our silly stories all over the world and it makes them smile on a good or bad day wrinkles my brain in the best kind of way. Having spent a lot of my life finding comfort in TV, music and podcasts, knowing that people turn to us in their times of need makes me so happy.

◎ Hearing a tram. One night, a few years ago, we were wrapping up a big night in the wee hours of the morning and I was sitting on the balcony, thinking about my mum. It must have been coming up to the anniversary of her death, and I was really emotional. I asked for a sign, and a tram dinged in the distance! I couldn't believe it. I asked for another sign and another tram trundled past across the bridge. I was telling a friend about it one night a while later and, all of a sudden, a tram pulled up right next to us. Whether you believe in that kind of thing or not, I love the little ways Mum can make me smile without even being here. It is so comforting.

◎ An incident from when Taubs and I were living in Sydney. We lived in this really cool part of town, lots of the other people in our apartment block were super cool and I was desperate to make friends. One afternoon, Taubs and I went and bought an embarrassing amount of KFC to feast on, and as we got home with our food, the cool people were walking down the stairs as we were walking up. Taubs stumbled and tripped on the stairs and the KFC bag ripped. The cool people helped us pick up our Potato & Gravy. We didn't catch up with them again.

◎ Listening to music really loudly in the car and having a singalong. I LOVE driving—I absolutely love it. There is nothing better than belting out a great tune while cruising around. It puts me in the best mood. Same goes for having a dance in the house in the morning. Nothing starts a day better than a dance in the kitchen.

◎ Having people over! I love playing host and having people over for breakfast, lunch, dinner, anything! I love the ritual of it—picking the food, doing a massive shop, putting music on, lighting a candle. An absolute dream.

◎ Hearing the coffee machine start while I'm still in bed. It means Taubs' face is about to pop into our bedroom and he's going to ask, 'Would you like a coffee, my love?'

◎ When someone tells me I look like my mum. I personally don't see it at all, so when people say it to me, it makes me so happy.

◎ Doing absolutely fuck-all, all day. I adore a 'nothing day', where I curl up on the couch and watch shitty reality TV. It doesn't happen as much as it used to, and I look forward to those days with Taubs. We call it nesting up.

◎ Buying gifts. Knowing I've thought about this thing for this person, or getting to say, 'I saw this and thought of you,' just makes my heart sing.

◎ Reminding myself how proud my mum was of me. When I was at school, I did lots of music subjects. I played the flute, I was in the senior band, I was the choir captain and I started studying classical voice. I was the only student studying performance opera, and Mum was so proud of me. I did singing lessons in the city every Tuesday night with a lovely woman called Catherine, and then Mum would take me for a sushi dinner afterwards. At my very first opera singing performance, Mum was in the crowd, filming, and screamed so loud. I still have the video saved on my desktop and watch it sometimes to hear her go 'YAAAY!! WOOOOO!' at the end. It's the only recording I have of her.

I love change and thrive on the unexpected, part two

I've mentioned how I and the rest of the Lodges really *thrive* on tradition. Every year, after we'd travelled to Broome for two weeks in July, and all of the birthdays had been celebrated the same way, Christmas would come.

In our house, Christmas started on 30 November. Dad would be in the backyard, grumbling about pulling the Christmas tree in from the shed. Boxes that were covered in spiders and whatever else had accumulated over the previous eleven months were stacked in the bar room of the house, ready for decorating on 1 December.

Christmas was Mum's favourite time of the year. She loved to spoil us, and loved the smiles and laughs, the hot weather, the food, the excuse for using fancy cutlery—everything.

For Mum, 1 December was almost as big as Christmas Day. I'd spend the day preparing with Mum, putting up tinsel and other Christmas decorations—including these little wicker sleighs that she'd fill with lollies, and refill throughout the month. We'd have a barbecue for dinner and we'd listen to Mum's favourite Christmas CD, which was called *Christmas Wishes*, an album of Christmas songs covered by Anne Murray and Kenny Rogers. At that point, it was time for the main event: putting up the Christmas tree.

Mum would hit play on that CD and it'd be game on. She would fold up a plastic, Christmas-themed tablecloth and lay it on the ground, then the tree would be assembled on top. There's nothing like the smell of a fake Christmas tree that's been in a box for almost a year.

Then we'd open the musty old plastic shopping bags full of tinsel, strings of beads, and so many other decorations Mum had bought or been gifted, or that we'd picked up along the way. There were these tiny golden bells that jingled every time one of the dogs walked past and their wagging tail knocked into the tree, and there was this glittery Jesus, Mary and Joseph decoration I'd always search for to place right on the front of the tree. It was massive and, oddly for us, very religious. I have no idea where it came from.

At the same time, there was music, Jamie eating lollies out of the wicker sleighs and throwing the wrappers at us, someone laughing, Mum singing along badly, and Dad swearing that the lights were all tangled and that 'we need a better system! This happens every year!' There was so much noise, but it was my favourite kind of chaos.

You know how when you're at a wedding, you're supposed to sneak a look at the groom while everyone else is looking at the bride? Like, it's this incredibly raw and delightful moment where no one else is looking at him, and his reaction and response is so true and special?

During this chaos, I'd be looking at Mum.

I have a mental album full of pictures of the smile that was pasted across her face while we laughed and argued about which side had too much tinsel or why we never had a theme. She'd watch all of us having fun, and I'd watch her taking it in.

The smiles only got bigger every year, and the family went in the same direction, growing with partners coming and going. The biggest smiles came when Jamie and Chelsea had their first baby. The first grandchild, the first nephew, Tyler.

Every Christmas as he got bigger, so did the smiles on all of our faces—but especially the one on Mum's. She adored Tyler, and he her. Mum never got mad or controlling over how the tree looked; it was always perfect to her, even if all of the decorations went in one spot, at Tyler-height.

• • •

The biggest honour that could have been bestowed on anyone in our family was putting Mum's beloved angel on the top of the tree.

It was the only time of the night when everything was quiet, and we'd all have a tear in our eye—pride for whoever was putting the angel on. Mum would always give a little speech about who she'd chosen to place the angel and why. The last year we put the tree up with Mum, she gave a speech about how the youngest member of our family, Jamie and Chelsea's daughter, Ashlee, would be putting the angel on the tree. Then, for the first time, we all overruled her.

We watched Dad hold Mum around the waist to support her while she delicately placed the angel on top of our beloved tree. Something that will stay with me forever.

After the decorations were finished, we'd turn on the lights of the Christmas tree (which had eventually been detangled), then turn off all the other lights in the house and walk across the road to admire our handiwork through the window. I remember Mum squeezing my hand every single year as we looked at the tree, and I could tell that her own mental album was filling up with pictures of that tree, flashing in the dark.

The month of December was the most colourful in our house, and the most fun. We would all be Christmas shopping and wrapping presents for each other, but Mum never put the presents from her and Dad out until after we'd gone to bed on Christmas Eve.

We'd put our Santa sacks on the end of our beds and force ourselves to sleep so that he would come.

On Christmas morning, we'd wake up so early and be so excited. I'd run into my sisters' rooms and we'd all compare what Santa had brought us—VERY QUIETLY—because it was still too early to wake up Mum and Dad, but we knew when we heard them put the kettle on that we were allowed to leave our end of the house.

We'd run out and look at all of the presents under the tree. Once a present was under there, it wasn't allowed to be touched until it was tree time. If something had been picked up, squeezed or moved—she'd know. It's where I learned self-restraint.

It was the most magical sight to see how Mum had laid everything out, to see all the effort and feel all the love in the house. I know not everyone gets that, so it's a very special memory for me.

We'd run into Mum's room and wake her up and squeal our Merry Christmas wishes, as Dad started breakfast.

Every single year would be the same. Dad would cook bacon, eggs, mushrooms and tomatoes on the barbecue and Mum would cook hash browns and croissants inside, while one of us would be whipping cream and pouring orange juice. Christmas breakfast was the only time we were allowed to use the gorgeous silver cutlery that spent the rest of the year tucked away in this gorgeous velvet lined, wooden box in the cupboard, so someone would also be wiping that before we could use it.

We'd eat breakfast, then we'd do the dishes together and run and make our beds, because not one single present could be touched until our beds were made. Sometimes we'd team up and while two of us did the dishes, the other two would make all the beds, so we could get to the presents quicker.

Then, like clockwork, we'd sit in front of the tree and Mum would hand out all of the presents. The first gift we opened was always undies—every single year. I don't know why, but it makes me laugh.

After the presents had been opened and we'd all compared treasures, Dad would head outside and check on the meat rotisserie that had been set up the night before, and Mum would put veggies on in preparation for our massive Christmas lunch. We'd eat off paper plates and after we were all finished, we threw the plates at the ceiling fan. I have NO idea why we did it, and whenever I tell people that, they give me this face that is a mix of 'Thank you for sharing that memory with me' and 'What the fuck?'

We'd clean up the mess and spend the afternoon swimming, napping, changing our outfits 100 times with the new clothes Mum and Dad had bought us (with Dad saying, 'That's nice, who got you that?' and us responding, 'You and Mum did!' and he'd lie and respond, 'Oh, of course, very nice!') until the evening, when Mum would put out platters of cold meat and cheese and chocolate and shortbread.

We'd spend the entire day at home, and extended family and friends would blow in throughout the day before moving on to the next family.

I loved our special Christmas traditions and never wanted them to end.

Then Mum passed away and I fell in love with Taubs, and all of a sudden, everything looked a bit different.

Taubs and I officially started dating in September, and we decided we should see each other on Christmas Day. A HUGE moment in a relationship, don't you think? Especially for me— I'd never left my house on Christmas Day, and all of a sudden I was not only going somewhere else, I was interrupting this perfectly balanced, smoothly flowing day where I knew exactly what I'd be eating and doing, by throwing another family into the mix.

But truthfully, I was just so excited to see my lovely, tall, brand-new boyfriend for Christmas.

• • •

Christmas now looks very different, which is something that gets a little bit easier every year. Taubs and I have spent Christmas alone in Japan, and we've spent Christmas with my incredible friend Jane's family in Albury. That Christmas with the Mackinlays was very special, and we spent the day eating, drinking and laughing, finishing up with a drunken game of Monopoly that took hours, before Taubs helped Jane's dad build a beehive he got for Christmas. Then Jane's mum said something that could have come from my own mum's mouth: 'It was just so lovely hearing you kids laughing and having fun.'

We've also spent Christmas with our best friends, Jag and Lain—just the four of us. We mixed their traditions with my favourite traditions, like having bacon, eggs and croissants for breakfast, and making sure the first present everyone opened on the day was fresh undies.

Because even though I LOVE change and thrive on the unexpected, let's not fix what's not broken.

Things I'd ask my mum if I could

◎ Do you want a coffee?

◎ How old were you when you lost your virginity?

◎ What order do you layer lasagne? Whenever I do meat on the bottom, it turns into a mess but pasta on the bottom doesn't seem right?

◎ Did you ever do drugs?

◎ How do you know when it's the right time to say, 'Yes!' or 'No!' or 'Fuck it, let's do it!'?

◎ When your mum passed away, were you as heartbroken as I am?

◎ What's the recipe for that mushroom gravy you used to make? And while we're here, how do you make your bacon and egg pie? I try to make it constantly and it turns to shit every frickin' time!

◎ Can we get another photo together?

◎ When did you get your first grey hair? Because I'm starting to get them and I'm wondering if it's too early or if it's normal. Also, my hair is totally changing texture, did that happen to you? It's gone wiry like pubes and I don't think that's right!

◎ Should I invest in laser hair removal? It's really expensive, but is it worth it?

◎ Where is your recipe for that marble cheesecake you used to make?

◎ How do I know if something makes me actually happy or just makes me smile? Is there a difference and does it matter?

◎ Where is my birth certificate?

I haven't met the Dalai Lama

Whenever I told people I worked in radio (and still now, when I tell people I used to work in radio), the first question would be, 'Which celebrities have you met?'

Aside from one time when I met Mel C from the Spice Girls—and totally fucked up an interview with her for *Jase & PJ*—the biggest celebrity encounter I've ever had happened long before I got into radio.

While I was studying sound engineering at WAAPA, I was also freelancing as an audio tech around Perth, trying to find odd jobs for some extra practical experience. The dream was to find enough work so I didn't have to do shifts in the Coles deli anymore, but until that happened, I was studying full time, working at Coles part time and freelancing in audio whenever I could get gigs.

I got this great job at another university (UWA—the University of Western Australia—which is, in fact, a university in Western Australia), and I was doing freelance audio with them fairly regularly. I did a whole range of stuff like mixing audio for music eisteddfods and graduations, setting up the sound for their writers' festival and putting microphones on people for conferences or lectures in their venues.

One day I was driving to a deli shift when I got a call from one of the managers at UWA, asking if I could come in as soon as possible because I had to get a photo taken for a police clearance. I explained that I already had my Working with Children Check, and they told me it was for something else—something highly confidential—relating to a shift I had coming up in a couple of weeks.

Very intrigued, I ventured into the office the following day to probe for more details. The venue manager told me the clearance was necessary for a very important speaking tour and, before I could say anything, added that it was NOT Oprah.

'It's the Dalai Lama. The 14th Dalai Lama, to be exact. He's coming to Perth and doing a talk at the university, so that's why we need a few different police clearances before we roster you on.'

I ended up passing the police clearances (obviously) and was very, very excited to work on this show. We were given a super strict briefing for our interaction with His Holiness the Dalai Lama—we weren't to talk to him or ask for photos or anything unprofessional. We were strictly to do what needed to be done and stay out of the way. No one working there had a reason to touch him or talk to him, anyway.

Except me!

I had to put on his microphone backstage, and show him the place from where he should walk onstage. Absolutely shitting myself about this responsibility, I waited backstage for him to arrive. The whole crew had been ready to go since about 6 a.m., ready for his arrival at 8 a.m., and the venue and entire university were crawling with police. Like, legit police, but also police in fancy suits instead of uniforms, like in *Men in Black*. Does that make them FBI or something?

Anyway, they were all walking around with earpieces in, talking into their sleeves, looking incredibly professional, and making me feel like I'd done something wrong. You know how when you're driving and you go through a random breath test and you're like, 'Oh my God, what if I accidentally put whiskey on my cereal this morning instead of milk and didn't notice?' Or when you're walking through the scanners at the airport and you think, 'Oh my God, what if I accidentally packed heroin and a bomb instead of my toiletries and extra undies?'

Just me? Cool, all good.

The Dalai Lama's scheduled arrival time of 8 a.m. came . . . and went. We were all getting very antsy about him not turning up. Maybe they got stuck somewhere and weren't going to make it? Maybe their flight had been delayed and it was all out of their control?

Then all of a sudden, the back doors of the venue swung open, six handsome and perfectly dressed security guards walked through saying 'the Eagle has landed' (not really) and behind them, a perfect circle of monks all walked in unison, surrounding His Holiness the Dalai Lama, followed by more suited police officers.

They were walking quickly to get onto the stage and instead of following the plan—for the Dalai Lama to stop and allow me to put his microphone on and direct him onstage—he walked straight out! Obviously, someone in the car had said, 'Look, DL, we're running a bit late, so just walk straight out, I reckon!'

The Dalai Lama walked out onto the stage and I heard an eruption of cheering that went beyond the crowds I've heard at AFL games or Lady Gaga's concerts. There was something so special about the energy in the room—it burned into sunshine and it was, for most of the people in the audience, a once-in-a-lifetime opportunity.

After letting myself get mixed up in the emotions of the room, I realised I was going to have to walk out onto the stage to put the Dalai Lama's microphone on.

I WANT TO BE FAMOUS, BUT NOT FOR THIS!

I was panicking more than I ever have. It was more of a panic than you have when you're doing a poo and have no toilet paper, more of a panic than when you're farting in front of your significant other for the first time—more of a panic than a random breath test or a walk through the airport scanners.

I was shitting myself.

There was also no 'boss' backstage who could tell me whether I was making the right call. I literally just had to decide that I was going to walk out there and possibly ruin the entire event.

I walked onto the stage to see the Dalai Lama greeting all the people in the front row, schmoozing away with no regard for little Toni Lodge, who needed to put on his microphone so she didn't get fired.

He finally walked towards his seat on the stage and I followed him there and smiled before politely stammering out, 'Excuse me, Your Holiness, I just need to put your microphone on, is that okay?' in front of an audience of about 55 million people. He smiled and said yes, and I placed his microphone behind his ears as the theatre went quiet.

In some ways, this day was no different from any other—aside from the obvious ways that it was completely different and never to be repeated—and so my hair was in its usual style, piled high in a bun on the top of my head. As he looked at me, His Holiness's face broke into a massive smile, and he said, 'Can I touch?', gesturing to my bun. I obviously obliged, and he gently grabbed my bun and went 'boop, boop, boop!' as the crowd broke out with laughter.

It was the most surreal and bizarre thing. I walked offstage, trying to figure out what had just happened.

The Dalai Lama and the student guild president who was interviewing him had a lovely conversation followed by a question-and-answer session which ran completely over time, to the point that His Holiness's posse were getting nervous about heading off on time. The Dalai Lama finally stood for the last round of applause and was whisked off the stage quickly to move on to his next event.

I was standing there at the ready to take off his microphone, and in the mix of craziness, he told me he loved my energy and held my hands in his with his eyes closed. It was such a beautiful experience. It was like all of the goodness of the universe was focused on me and my soul. Like staring right into the sun but without those little black dots ruining your vision after.

I was so excited to get home and tell Taubs and all of my family about it. I gave them the long version of events, and then someone tagged me in a video on Facebook saying, 'Toni is this you?!'

And lo and behold—the video was of His Holiness the 14th Dalai Lama and me onstage together! Except right as it gets to the bit where he played with my hair, the video cuts and transitions to him sitting down! You hear the crowd laughing, but you miss him playing with my hair!

Maybe it was a fever dream and it didn't happen? Maybe this is the only lie in this book that's *actually* a lie?

NO! It definitely happened! I SWEAR ON THIS BOOK!

I don't need therapy, part three

You've learned now that I know how to deal with my emotions. Hahahahahaha. Another lie for you—that one's for free.

After not getting help at any of the major milestones I've mentioned so far, where therapy was definitely required, I now look back on a pattern which I repeat to this day. When life gets tough and I'm faced with the opportunity, or *necessity*, to go through therapy or face some of my demons, I throw myself into work.

Even right now, it's Friday night and I'm supposed to be at a work party. I'm dressed up in the chic uniform of jeans and a nice top, I've curled my hair, brushed out my eyebrows and put on shoes . . . and now I'm sitting at my computer, writing this book.

Let me step you through my routine.

1.00 p.m. Complain about needing to go to the party and talk myself into having a shower and washing my hair.

1.30 p.m. Actively decide I will not be going, but am thankful I have washed my hair because it's done for the weekend now.

1.45 p.m. Feel guilty for not living my life and decide no, I will go, actually!

2.00 p.m. Start to have feelings of anxiety and want to stay home, but remind myself how much fun it will be. Tell myself I'll work for another hour and then get ready, to be there by four o'clock.

3.00 p.m. Decide I'll use my Airwrap to curl my wet hair; an appliance I haven't used to curl my hair before, so will take 100 years and probably look shit. Hair ends up looking great and I'm 'really happy about it'.

3.30 p.m. Put on brand-new jeans and nice top and feel too fat to go to the party.

3.35 p.m. Actively hate the way that I look so much that I give myself a tummy ache and really don't want to go.

3.40 p.m. No, actually! I'm cool! I'm more than what I look like! I'm going!

3.45 p.m. Realise I need to go to the bottle shop on the way to the party, so maybe I shouldn't go?

3.50 p.m. Decide I'll go to the bottle shop and then get an Uber to the party and have fun! I'll get a bottle of champagne to celebrate with everyone! Not celebrating anything in particular, but just happy to be here!!!

3.55 p.m. Stand at the door with one shoe on and one shoe off, trying to decide what to do.

3.57 p.m. Get angry that I hate the way I look.

4.05 p.m. Taubs asks what time I have to be there and I say four o'clock and he says, 'Well, you better get a wriggle on!'

4.06 p.m. Ryan calls me and asks me a question about the podcast and I decide there's no way I can possibly go out because I have far too much work to do.

Let's have a look at that last time check-in on that Get Ready with Me play-by-play. Throwing myself into work as a barrier to avoid my problems.

I am excuses central. I make excuses for myself all the time. 'I can't do this because I can't afford it', 'I can't do that because I don't have time', 'I can't do the other because I'm too busy'.

At the last junction of 'not needing therapy', I was suffering an affliction so severe that I likened it to being shot, and a very lovely cardiologist told me it was caused by grief. I was told in no uncertain terms that it would continue if I didn't try to face it, and that my physical and mental health would both suffer if I kept ignoring it.

Instead, I got a new job. This was the beginning of my career in radio, and there's nothing like beginning an entirely new career and moving your life to a new city to take your mind off your litany of mental health issues! (If anyone needs life advice, give me a call.)

As I moved from city to city, working in radio and changing my life and address more often than some people change their underwear, I kept pushing down any feelings of grief, depression and anxiety, because I was just so *busy*.

I would tell myself I was happy, which technically *wasn't* a lie, because day to day, I probably was pretty happy! But the real feelings were deep in my tummy.

The landscape around the hustle and the grind is slowly changing. The social media obsession with 'rise and grind' and 'girl boss' and 'make muscle, make hustle' (I made up the last one) is fading away. Now, it's all about taking time on a Sunday to sleep in and snuggling your designer dog and setting your phone to Do Not Disturb while you watch Netflix at night instead of replying to emails.

But I don't think I am the way that I am because of Instagram and girl bosses. I think I just know what's inside me. Even now, I'm just not ready to see that sadness spill out of my eyes and then mouth and then seep through every pore in my face. And I certainly wasn't then. So working and keeping busy was the answer.

• • •

Promotions and postcode changes took us eventually to Sydney for six months, as I've written, and I should have been so excited and so happy, but I was so fucking depressed. Taubs and I had *no* money, our apartment was super old and freezing cold (and $600 a week), and I was working weekdays from

2 p.m. till around 10 p.m. Every morning, I would wake up when Taubs was going to work and just sit in the house until 1 p.m., then go into work where I'd be super busy before the night show aired. Then everyone else would finish up their day at a normal hour, while I had to work in the office by myself from around 6 p.m. until 10 p.m., which was so lonely, apart from the twenty minutes around 8 p.m. when the cleaners would buzz around.

I'd get home from work and Taubs would have waited to cook and eat dinner with me, so we would eat around 11 p.m. then slip straight into bed. It was really crap.

The funny, hot, sick feeling started to return every day while I was getting ready for work, now with the addition of chest pains. I'd cry on the phone to my brother most nights when I was driving home from work, and I'd say, 'I can't fucking do this.'

He'd say, 'Yes, you can. I've seen you do things that no one else can, so you can do anything. But you don't *have* to do this, if you don't want to.'

I kept doing it, though. I worked really hard to get there, and even though it wasn't quite right for me, I knew something was coming. The Lodge Magic would strike again!

Then a miracle was dropped on top of me, and I got the job in Melbourne at *Jase & PJ*.

• • •

Again, knowing I could distract myself from the grey feelings that were overtaking all of the colour in my life, we packed up and moved to Melbourne, exhausting what little savings we'd rebuilt in the six months we'd been in Sydney (and then some).

New city, new job, new challenges, new distractions, right? When you start a new job, you know there'll be that buffer period of around two or three months where you're not sick of it and the excitement hasn't worn off and you don't hate anyone you work with yet.

The job at *Jase & PJ* was a complete lifestyle change. I was working from 4.30 a.m. or 5 a.m. every morning right up until the job was done. Sometimes it was 11 a.m., sometimes it was 2 p.m., sometimes it was 9 p.m. Don't know about you, but for me, that equals having too many working hours to deal with my emotions and being too tired to feel depressed. Right?

But the two- or three-month buffer period came and went and the grey feelings were back, sucking the colour out of my life and personality at a rapid speed.

This is where my obsession with time started to take a terrifying shape. My life was ruled by the clock. Knowing I had to be strict about what time I woke up because of how early I had to start work meant I had to be strict about what time I went to bed, what time I ate dinner, what time I woke up from falling asleep on the couch in the afternoon—everything.

I've talked about my obsession with time, and this job just threw me into overdrive. I tried to train my body to be tired the moment the clock hit 8.30 p.m., and when that didn't work and I couldn't sleep, I would cry all night about how useless

I was, and work myself up over how much sleep I wouldn't get. Like an overtired baby who can't articulate their problem, I would just bawl my eyes out until my skin was raw and cry myself into a coma.

I would obsessively check my alarm each night until it felt 'right'. I'd check it and close the app on my phone, check it again and close the app again, then check it again and close the app and reopen it until my brain accepted that it was switched on and I wouldn't sleep in. Then I'd wake up periodically through the night, every hour or so, and repeat the same routine.

I'd check the door was locked, check the oven was off and check the balcony door was locked, over and over until I felt at ease. That would waste so much time, I'd start to cry at how much I wanted to sleep, but I couldn't until it felt *right*.

I know, we're all thinking it: everyone has lain in bed, looking at the clock and thought, 'If I get to sleep RIGHT NOW, I will get exactly seven hours and that's okay!' but this was a whole other ball game.

On a bad night, I would get so panicked that I'd hyperventilate until I'd throw up. I'd keep checking the time, keep checking my alarm and keep crying. I'd get so hot that I'd have to have a shower to calm down. And as you can imagine, all of THAT takes up a lot of fucking time. If I'd just meditated or something, I would have got way more sleep. (Hindsight is 20/20 after all!)

• • •

One night, around a week before the anniversary of my mum's death (which is our family's worst week of the year), I couldn't sleep.

I did the same old routine as described above, the panic attack, blah blah blah ... and Taubs was sitting in bed with me, trying to calm me down. Then, all of a sudden, through the snot and tears and anxiety and sadness, I heard him ask me the simplest question I've ever been asked.

'Do you like feeling this way?'

Like, I'm sitting here covered in my own snot and he's deciding THIS is the right time for a fucking intervention?! 'Of course not! Who would like feeling like this?' I barked back. 'Who would want to feel so out of control of their body and life that every second that slips past feels like a lifetime?' I cried. 'This isn't the time!' And then I said, 'Hang on ... what is time?' And I started thinking to myself, I have to wake up at 4.30 a.m. and I'm gonna be tired whether I get eight hours sleep or four hours sleep, because it's still dark when I wake up! If I tell my body right now that it's 8.30 p.m., will it really know the difference? Is my brain actually *that* smart?

Yes, my brain had tricked me into grief-induced chest pains, but maybe ... I could trick it right back. Like when you're playing hide-and-seek with a child and you see a massive lump under a blanket and you can hear them giggling and you say, 'OH, I GUESS THEY'RE NOT IN HERE!' Could I trick my brain in the same way? Would it fall for it?

Then I realised that I was fighting my brain, every step of the way. It was an us-and-them mentality, with my brain being smarter than me, but my brain *is* me, and *I'm* my brain.

Could we work together? Could I use the power of my brain for good, not evil? Would my brain help my body to get better instead of warring with it? Would my brain ever forgive me for the lies?

And in that snot-covered aha moment, I knew. Time may just be a construct, but I decided right then that I didn't want to waste another fucking second of it feeling the way I did in my bed that night, crying over my iPhone screen telling me it was 1 a.m.

It was a very weird moment. My brain took my hand and I felt like the two halves of me were reconnected for the first time since they'd been ripped apart by my mental health struggles. The slow tear of being bullied by the big kids on the bus, every time I got overly defensive, each and every single self-loathing thought, every boy who didn't like me, every time I'd stood in front of the mirror and hated my body, and each second without my mum—each time a stitch of the fabric of my life had popped open and I had bullied myself out of my own relationship with myself.

'I need therapy. I can't do this anymore.'

The next day, I went to my GP and asked for a mental health assessment and a mental health plan. This gave me access to ten subsidised therapy sessions for the year, and I got a referral to a therapist.

I got really lucky with an appointment coming up shortly after I'd received my referral, and I was able to go in and meet my new best friend, Dr Therapist*. (*Okay obviously his name is not Dr Therapist, but I'm not going to share his name, it's already hard enough to get an appointment.)

I caught an Uber to my first session despite it being one tram ride away from my house. The ride cost a fortune, but I was too stressed to tackle more than one trauma centre in one day. I walked in and sat down in the waiting room, sweating bullets while smelling fresh coffee from the kitchenette and listening to the soft chatter of Brené Brown coming from a YouTube playlist of her videos on the waiting room TV.

The thing that had put me off going to therapy in the past was breaking the ice—the question of 'why are you here?' that they show on every TV show when the characters go to therapy for the first time, or the couch opposite the therapist that you're not sure whether you should sit or lie down on. Then there's the sterile fact of telling your darkest secrets to a stranger and then them asking you for money; or, the worst part, splitting your emotional wounds open and splaying your sadness across the room only for them to ask you to leave when your allocated hour is over, no matter where you've gotten up to in your life story. Basically, I was anxiously trying to plan out an hour-long conversation with someone I'd never met.

• • •

A young, well-dressed man walked down the hallway and asked me to follow him into his office. There was an armchair for me to sit in, so I didn't have to decide whether to sit up or lie down, and he didn't ask, 'Why are you here?'

Instead, he asked me about my day and if I'd found the place okay, and told me straight off the bat he would never let me leave the office if I wasn't feeling safe or ready to go. After that, the conversation flowed and my hour was over in the blink of an eye. He didn't ask me for any money. He told me that everything was done via email, after my appointment, for me to deal with when I was ready.

This part sounds like a lie, but Dr Therapist changed my life. The understanding, the care, the support and the listening that I didn't realise I needed. Working through my anxiety, depression and a diagnosis of OCD, I felt my body, my subconscious and my brain holding hands so tightly, and my life felt like it was in full bloom. This was the opening up and rebirth of Toni Lodge.

This whole time, I'd been smiling at work and making jokes with my friends and lying about how great I felt. But the smiles were becoming truer and more authentic every day. The colour slowly flowed back into my life and I felt the change through every part of my body and all of my relationships.

After a while, I started feeling so confident that I stopped getting Ubers to my appointments, catching the tram instead and enjoying my afternoons of self-care. Then, after seeing Dr Therapist every fortnight for almost a year, we started spacing my appointments further apart, and eventually it got to the point where I didn't have anything to talk to him about and he'd send me home early and each time I'd feel happy and proud of myself.

One day, I walked into my appointment and Dr Therapist asked how I was.

I said, 'I'm really good!' and for the first time in what felt like forever, I genuinely meant it. It wasn't a lie. I wasn't 'good' in the way you tell the person at Coles you're 'good' as they scan your groceries, and it wasn't the same 'good' you say to a relative you don't really care for, but a genuine 'good', in every sense of the word.

And he said, 'Toni, I don't think you need me anymore. Of course, I'll always be your therapist, and you can lean on me as often as you need to or would like to, but you don't need these regular appointments anymore.'

I was stunned. As my eyes welled up with tears, I said, 'I feel like you're breaking up with me. Is that normal?'

Dr Therapist said, 'That's completely normal, but the fact you've articulated that to me shows me you're ready for this.' And he reassured me that this was NOT a breakup, and I was welcome to come back whenever I needed him.

I caught the tram home feeling a strange mixture of heartbreak and elation. I remember walking in the door and telling Taubs what had happened, then bawling my eyes out while saying I was so proud of myself. It was a really messy, really beautiful moment of pride and of coming full circle. All that time spent in my apartment, wasting time crying over wasted time until blood vessels burst in my eyes, to realising I needed therapy, to now, crying in my apartment because I was so proud of how far I'd come.

It was around 4 p.m. I made myself a coffee and sat on the balcony, shaking, trying to remind myself the tears were good tears, and not a taste of the old lies.

• • •

After spending the night unpacking my feelings and assessing how I felt about everything, the next day, I decided I needed to say thank you.

I had so much to say to Dr Therapist that I decided was too sincere and heartfelt for an email. So, after work, I went to Coles and bought a cute thank-you card and passed by the florist and bought a cactus in a gorgeous ceramic pot. We all know the type of person I am, and that in my sincerest moments I need to cut back to my core and make a joke, so the heartfelt card accompanying the plant ended with a pun that thanked him for helping me 'grow'.

I jumped in the car and drove through a busy part of town to Dr Therapist's office, a chic little house turned into a therapy clinic on a one-way side street. I very quickly pulled over to the side of the road. The plan was to sprint up the steps, leave the plant and card at the door so as not to interrupt anyone's appointment, and jump back in the car.

So, I ran over the road in my white platform sneakers . . . and tripped on the decking steps, sending myself headfirst into the door, plant in hand. Face-planting, if you will.

Worse, the door opened just as I was about to launch through it, and I tripped headfirst into Dr Therapist's crotch. So I had to explain to a very confused guy who had 'broken up' with me why I was on his doorstep, in his crotch, holding a little cactus.

Turns out Dr Therapist was right: I didn't need therapy anymore! But after that encounter, he probably does.

I know where our passports are at all times

I met Taubs when we were at uni together. We were studying the same thing and I don't think he really liked me much at first. Not just romantically—at all. I was in the year above him and when we had to work on theatre shows together, I was 'in charge' of the team.

I'll be the first to admit that I'm not a good manager. I get stressed, I'm not great at explaining things or teaching people, and it's just not my jam. Taubs denies it now, but I'm pretty sure he thought I was a massive bossy boots and probably bitched about me to the other guys on our team.

I was well aware of my weakness as a team leader, so I was probably trying to butter him up. This one night on a show, I had to grab some more gear from the studio—a task that definitely didn't need two people—and I asked him to come and give me a hand. Taubs is probably one of the smartest people in the world, so I really respected him. But he was older than me because he'd studied other things at a different uni (I did mention he's probably one of the smartest people in the world, remember!) so I felt weird about being 'in charge'.

While we were walking back from the studio, we passed a rehearsal room where a bunch of dancers were blasting the song 'Midnight City' by M83. I started dancing (because that song is FUCKING great) and turned to Taubs, expecting him to be staring at me weirdly, but he was dancing too!

'I LOVE this song!' I yelled.

And he yelled, 'Yeah, M83 are fantastic.'

Then I copped a whiff of him and said, 'You smell like cinnamon scrolls!', which is a fucking weird thing to say.

And he said, 'Yeah, its Old Spice.'

That night, we finished a little later than expected and I knew where he lived because I was friends with one of his housemates. It was *kind of* on my way home (if I went a different way home) so I asked if he wanted a ride to save him catching the bus.

It was almost midnight and we hadn't eaten any dinner, so we went through the Macca's drive-through and he offered me some spare change and a $5 note to pay me back and I told him not to worry about it. I remember being so fucking hungry and Taubs fed me some chips as I was driving.

It was the first time we'd really gotten chatting. We shared our love for Meatloaf (the singer) and we laughed a lot.

We had two weeks left on the show and from then on I picked him up for uni more often than not, and would drop him off most nights too. We became legit friends. We'd text when we weren't together and when we were together, we were inseparable. We just had so much fun and laughed so much.

When we then became kissing friends, it felt like it made so much sense. The ease of turning such an amazing friendship into smooching just felt so simple. Like when someone offers you a chip from their plate: it's easy. It makes sense. There's only one answer.

Inside the sound department at WAAPA, there were 30 of us across the first, second and third years. It was the same across the board for the lighting, costume and stage management departments, as well as actors and musical theatre students— everyone. It meant we were a relatively small and close-knit cohort, especially within our own departments.

It also meant it got pretty bloody awkward when people slept together. So, to make sure everyone was kept happy, if someone from the sound department slept with someone in a different department, they had to buy the rest of the sound team a cake. It was always a Coles Mud Cake, and it made the interdepartmental awkwardness 'worth it'.

However, if someone from sound slept with someone else from sound, the sex-havers had to purchase an ice-cream cake as compensation. I guess the logic was that an ice-cream cake was WAY more expensive and SO much yummier.

No one from uni really thought much of Taubs and me hanging out, I don't think. We would always rock up to class together, arrive at parties together and leave together, but no one said anything.

Then, one night we were all at a party at our mate Tech Deck's house, and I wasn't going to drink, so of course I picked Taubs up on my way to the party. After a couple of hours, everyone got super loose and I decided to head home. Taubs and I said goodbye to everyone and we hopped in the car and went on our merry way.

When we got back to Taubs' house, I saw I had a missed call from Christian, one of the guys still at the party, and he'd left a voicemail. We listened to it on speakerphone in the car, and it started with Christian calmly saying, 'Hey Toni, it's Christian, I'd just like to let you know I have my suspicions about you and Taubs sleeping together,' but eventually turned into twenty of our drunk friends saying, 'WE KNOW YOU GUYS ARE DOING IT WITH EACH OTHER AND YOU OWE US A CAKE!'

Taubs and I looked at each other and realised we'd been sprung, so the following Monday morning, we stopped at Coles on the way to uni and bought two Freddo Party Cakes—one each. (Cheaper than buying one for each time we'd done it!)

We walked down into the area behind the sound building, where we all sat between classes (which I had built actually. It's called 'The Sound Lounge' and it is my personal victory and legacy. What began as us picking up couches off the side of the road during hard rubbish collections turned into hundreds of emails between the heads of the university and me, and eventually ended in our getting proper cemented park benches) and presented the team with two ice-cream cakes for breakfast. We weren't actually officially dating by this point, so everyone loved making it awkward—but we'd done the crime and we'd pay the price.

After a while of us sleeping together, I eventually asked Taubs out for real and we were boyfriend and girlfriend. (An awkward conversation, but luckily worked out in my favour!) I don't think anyone (including us) ever expected it to turn into an actual relationship, and it's so wild to think about.

Whenever I think about how lucky I am, I also think how lucky the rest of our sound team are that we never broke up while we were still at uni—that would have been fucking insufferable.

We worked awesomely as a team. We never fought, we were never unprofessional, and our dynamic made us super efficient as a couple too. Some power did go to my head, though, when a Facebook page where students posted anonymous things about WAAPA posted a message from someone saying they loved seeing the 'power couple strutting around WAAPA', which I can ONLY assume was about us. But I think we truly are the definition of a power couple, because we really are the best team. Professionally, personally, in the house, out of the house, in a crisis—we're fucking switched on.

It has made lots of tough times much easier. Like travelling.

• • •

I am not a good traveller. Not because I'm a bad flyer—like, I don't get sick or anything—but I do get really stressed about travelling and forgetting something, missing a flight or bus, or having to run in the airport. All of those things are just not my ideal situation. I'm not very fit and the idea of sprinting through an airport is such a nightmare—unless of course there is a camera crew involved and a laugh to be had, then I'm your gal. I hate feeling stressed or pressured, so travelling just makes me so anxious. If Taubs is flying without me, I watch the flight tracker the entire time until he lands safely.

But the great thing about being such a fantastic team is that we both know our strengths. I like to be prompt, so I am happy to be the person who decides what time we leave. Taubs doesn't get flapped easily and is much fitter than me, so he's happy to lead the way navigation-wise and to carry the bags. I like to be organised, so I always have the printed itinerary and the travel wallet with our spare cash and emergency credit card, printouts of our passports with all the important numbers and, of course, our actual passports.

While we were at uni, we went on a trip to Vietnam. You know how they say the first trip together is very telling? Well, we didn't live together yet, and it was a huge test of our relationship. You would think we would have dipped a toe in the waters with maybe a car trip or overnight staycation, but instead, we flew from Perth to Vietnam and stayed for a whole week. It went perfectly. The system of me holding the documents and Taubs navigating worked like clockwork and we lived to tell the tale.

After we moved in together, we decided to go on another trip, this time to Japan to visit some of Taubs' friends and see the sights. It was the middle of winter, so I was also hoping to see snow for the first time!

This trip was a bit different, because instead of flying there and staying put, we travelled around for three weeks, and we weren't in any one place for longer than four or five days before moving on to the next place via train. All the packing and unpacking was a lot for this poor little traveller! We weren't fighting or anything, but I was feeling so anxious and I really wanted to just settle somewhere for longer.

This one day in particular, we were travelling from one city to the next, so we headed to the train station. We were both carrying big hiking backpacks, and Taubs was also carrying a regular backpack with our water bottles and books and snacks. After walking through the train station, I was too hot in my big woolly overcoat, so I was carrying that in my hands, along with the travel wallet that had our train passes.

Because I despise being late, we ended up down on the train platform half an hour early, so we sat down. There was a train sitting there, and we decided that until that one left and ours rocked up, we would take off our backpacks and settle in.

About 27 minutes later, this train hadn't left yet, meaning that ours hadn't come, and just as it was about to close its doors, the information screen on the side of the train flicked over to display the details of the train we were ABSOLUTELY SUPPOSED TO BE ON. And in a mad dash, we sprinted onto the train that had been sitting there, with us right next to it, for half an hour.

We ended up just making it onto the train, which took off about twelve seconds after we piled onto it. I was in an absolute tizz.

Around 55 minutes later, we were nearing the station where we were getting off and I decided to get all our stuff together to make sure we didn't leave anything behind. I grabbed the small backpack with our water bottles and snacks to put my book away and get the travel wallet with our train passes.

Even now, years later, I'd bet good fucking money on me having put the travel wallet into that backpack. I'd put the house on it. I swear I remember stuffing it in there. But it wasn't there.

Perplexed, but not yet panicked, I looked around us to see if it had slipped onto the floor or beneath our seats during the trip—but the travel wallet was nowhere to be seen.

I grabbed Taubs' attention. 'Hey, the passports aren't here, do you have them?' I asked, and he shook his head.

I started to panic. The travel wallet definitely wasn't on the floor of the train or in the small backpack, and we were pulling up to our stop. We needed to get off or we'd end up on the opposite side of the country, so Taubs grabbed our big hiking backpacks down from the racks and I stood in the door of the train with one foot on the platform and one foot inside the carriage so it couldn't take off.

At this point, I was absolutely hysterical. I pulled everything out of our bags in the middle of the station—books, knickers, clothes, toiletries, makeup, towels. Every single thing in those bags was now on the platform of a Japanese train station.

But not our fucking passports.

Not speaking a lick of Japanese, aside from pleasantries, we tried to tell the person who was supposed to check our tickets to let us out that I'd misplaced them along with our passports and emergency money. It was really difficult, not because of the language barrier, but because I was screaming and crying and hyperventilating at this lovely young woman who actually spoke English perfectly well.

I felt so ashamed. I'd let the team down. We each had our jobs: Taubs carried the bags and navigated our way, and I told the time and looked after the passports. I had failed at my job and I was so devastated to fuck our trip up in this way. I apologised profusely to Taubs, who stayed calm and said, 'Don't worry, we'll find them!'

I'd decided that we needed to go to the Australian Consulate and get emergency passports. I started crying again about how much that would cost because, like all uni students who have ever travelled, we had a very limited emergency budget, and all of that budget was in a very safe spot. Which happened to be the travel wallet. Which was now lost.

After the longest 45 minutes of my whole life, the lovely young woman, who had been helping us and calling people to ascertain the whereabouts of our travel wallet, gave us a thumbs up. She hung up the phone to tell us they had found it.

'Oh my GOD! Thank you! Are our passports in there? Are our train passes in there? IS OUR MONEY IN THERE?!' I asked calmly.

'We aren't allowed to open lost property, I'm sorry, so I'm not sure.'

We had to travel an hour backwards by train (and buy new tickets), hoping on a wing and a prayer that someone hadn't just taken all the good stuff out, stolen our identities and ditched the empty wallet.

I was still hyperventilating when we got back to that train station. I sprinted through the station to lost property, and the man working there took one look at me and said, 'I think this is yours?' before presenting the travel wallet.

I burst into tears and thanked him over and over again before the moment of truth. I unzipped the travel wallet . . . and found our printed itinerary, all of our cash, our emergency credit card, the printed versions of our passports and, of course, our actual passports.

I started crying again (I hadn't stopped, really) and thanked the man over and over once again, and also silently thanked my mum for looking out for us and our passports. Of all the awful things I've experienced through grief, there have been some special moments too, that have made me feel really connected to Mum. Whether it's a song she loved randomly coming on while I'm in the car, or a last-minute solution showing itself in a pinch. It's a bit like the Lodge Magic.

I looked at Taubs and apologised so many times for letting the team down. And instead of saying, 'Oh my love, don't worry, we found them!' which I assumed he would, he smirked and said, 'Now that we have them back, I have two things to say. First, I didn't think we'd get those back, and also,' his smile grew, 'I am so fucking glad it was you who lost them and not me.'

We both laughed and I choked on my tears and thanked my lucky stars for having such a great teammate.

Dr Toni Lodge

About fifteen years ago, I signed up for a Myer one card. Myer is a big department store, and Myer one is a free loyalty program where you get a physical, plastic card sent to your house. Being thirteen or fourteen, I got such a kick out of having proper plastic cards in my wallet and feeling like a grown-up, so when I saw the pamphlet in Myer, I couldn't resist. There was a website where you could sign up, and I was so fucking excited that I rushed through the registration, hit submit and waited by the letterbox until the card arrived.

It finally came, and my eyes lit up as soon as I saw the Myer logo on the envelope. Then my eyes clocked the name on the address: Dr Toni Lodge.

Confused, I opened it up. Printed on the letter AND the card was Dr Toni Lodge.

In my excitement, I had scrolled past 'Miss' on the drop-down prefix menu and selected 'Dr'.

I understand that with great power comes great responsibility. If I was on a plane and a flight attendant screamed, 'IS THERE A DOCTOR ON BOARD?' I would, obviously, NOT say yes.

However, I'm giving myself permission here and now to write some prescriptions. These are like blank cheques—cash whichever one you need, as many times as you need.

Dr Toni Lodge, I need my boyfriend to open up and cry in front of me!

Watch *How I Met Your Mother*, season 9, episodes 23 and 24. These are the final episodes, where the whole season wraps up. No spoilers, but if you know, you know. I watched them with Taubs, and we sat on the floor in his room bawling our eyes out for hours. It wasn't long after my mum had died and it was just so real and raw. Every time I watch it, I remember the smell of the house we were in. It was the first time I saw Taubs cry. The second time I saw him cry, however, was at my mum's grave. So if you have one of those at your disposal, that will also work.

Dr Toni Lodge, I'd like to laugh uncontrollably in an inappropriate manner!

Watch *Modern Family*, season 9, episode 1. This is the episode when they're all on the cruise for the eclipse and Cam is travelling back to the ship on a dinghy. He's dressed in a massive white gown for sun protection and the dinghy's propellor rips it off and he squeals. I have watched it 3,903,704 times and I lose it laughing every single time.

Dr Toni Lodge, I'd love to laugh and feel things and then bawl my eyes out on a train in Japan!

Read *Why Not Me?* by Mindy Kaling. When Taubs and I were in Japan (not long after I lost AND FOUND our passports), we were travelling by train and I was behaving like a main character by reading a paperback book and listening to my iPod. I got to a part in the book where Mindy describes her feelings around being scared that, since her mum had passed away, she'd forget what her voice sounds like. It sent a chill down my spine and made me sob in front of many businessmen.

Dr Toni Lodge, I'd like to laugh and cry while watching the second-most-perfect Australian TV show.

Watch *Please Like Me*, season 3, episode 2. I would prescribe every single episode of *Please Like Me* by Josh Thomas, but in particular the episode where Josh's stepmum, Mae, tells Josh's dad that she's had an affair with a guy she met on the internet. And Josh's dad says, 'The bloody internet? I'm sick of it!' in a very dad way. Hilarious. (Side note: the first-most-perfect Australian TV show is obviously *Kath and Kim*.)

Dr Toni Lodge, I'd like to forget about the outside world and sing/dance in the car until my voice hurts.

Listen to 'Welcome to the 60s' from *Hairspray*. Mum and I used to smash this in the car whenever we were driving together. Any musical theatre soundtrack will do the trick here, but this is a personal fave.

Listen to 'Woman' by Kesha. A fucking BELTER song to smash in the car. You will never live life the same way after listening to this loudly while driving. I have strutted into workplaces I didn't want to be in after smashing this. You never regret it.

Listen to 'The Best' by Tina Turner. For obvious reasons, this song is a fantastic vibe-setter. When my mum was pregnant with me, she and my dad went to a Tina Turner concert and apparently, I was bouncing around and going mental the entire time. When Tina sang this, she would pick one person in the crowd to sing to and that night, it happened to be my dad. (A special mention should go to *Schitt's Creek* for giving this song a whole new meaning.)

Dr Toni Lodge, I'd like to fall more in love with rockstars that I've been in love with for my whole life.

Read *Can I Say* by Travis Barker. After Travis Barker started dating Kourtney Kardashian, I feel like he slid back into our hearts—but he NEVER left mine. I assume Blink-182 listens went right up on Spotify when that happened, and if you'd like to intensify your crush on this handsome guy, read his book. It's very good.

Read *Scar Tissue* by Anthony Kiedis. Another verrry good auto-biography that just made me fall completely in love with him even more than I already was.

Read *Rob Delaney: Mother. Wife. Sister. Human. Warrior. Falcon. Yardstick. Turban. Cabbage.* by Rob Delaney. A special mention to Rob Delaney, who is *not* a rockstar, but this is a fantastic book that gave me that 'I need more of you!' feeling that I HOPE you get from this book.

Dr Toni Lodge, I'd love for my boyfriend's friends to not really like me straight away.

Play *ANY FUCKING BOARD GAME*. The first time I ever met all of Taubs' friends was at a 'low-key' games night, and I wanted to impress them all and play it cool. But I've never played anything cool in my whole life, and when I play board games I get very yell-y. Realising I needed to rein it in, I knew that when all else failed, I could be funny and charming. Then we started playing Cards Against Humanity and my last-ditch attempt at being 'the funny one' didn't work. I cried on the way home and never wanted to see them again. We get along now, though. I think.

Dr Toni Lodge, I'd like to listen to the funniest podcast in the world.

Listen to *Toni and Ryan*. I've heard this podcast is very good and very popular.

I don't want to be famous, part two

I've had lots of 'midlife' crises.

My first one was in Year 10, when I freaked out that I didn't know where I belonged and that every day of my life was going to look exactly the same. Sitting on the ground outside the library, my group of besties talked me through it.

The second one happened during my gap year. I couldn't decide what I wanted to do at uni and felt panicked because the reason I took a year off was to save money, but I had struggled to find a job. I'd ended up working at a fish market that was VERY far away from my house, and then quitting that job for a boyfriend who didn't end up being worth quitting a job for. I was stressed that I'd given away a fun job and couldn't find another, had no money to show for it and didn't know what I should study. But I cried to Mum and then found a different job at General Pants and lived to tell the tale. I also got into WAAPA—a great year for me in the end!

The third crisis was while I was at uni. I was stressed that I had picked the wrong course and would never be able to find a job or do anything that made me truly happy. I was scared that I'd never be able to make good money, that I'd never have a stable life. I had just moved out of home, so that probably had a role to play too. Sitting together on our bed, Taubs talked me through it.

He locked me in our room with an empty notebook and said, 'Take half an hour to yourself and write down your wildest dreams, and see what comes out!' When the time was up, Taubs opened the door to a sobbing Toni and a still-empty notebook— I had continued to stress that I'd never find my spot. But we ended up talking through it, and I said my ideal job would be one where I laughed all day, every day, and made a living being able to make people laugh.

The fourth crisis was when we lived in Sydney. Stressed to death because I'd left an easy job in WA where my family was and where rent was cheaper, I was devastated about leaving my friends and felt bad about dragging Taubs with me, first to Sydney and now to Melbourne. I was also used to being a bigger fish in a smaller pond and, all of a sudden, I was a tiny fish in a MASSIVE pond, and my dreams of being famous were kind of dashed. How could I make an impact in a place with millions of other talented people?

• • •

When I started working at *Jase & PJ*, I laughed all day, every day.

It wasn't me making people laugh, but I did get to laugh along with a group of my new best buds, so I thought, 'This is probably as good as it's gonna get, and it's pretty fucking great!'

I was enjoying finally finding my spot and I was working hard, so happy to have found something that was stable, but still different every day.

But after a while, I felt a little unfulfilled.

I was having fun and getting to work in a super supportive and creative environment, but I wanted to be the one doing the talking and making people laugh. After getting a taste of it from working on Jase and PJ's podcast and making videos for the team, I was hungry for it: hungry for that feeling you get when you perform and make people laugh, which I can only imagine is the same feeling marathon runners refer to as 'runners' high'.

I was working for the talent, but I wanted to be the talent.

Then, at a weird time in life, something crazy happened. The Lodge Magic came to visit! We were a couple of months into Covid-19 lockdowns, so creativity was at this all-time low and everyone seemed to be just getting by. I was asked to go on a podcast called *The Daily Talk Show*. The guys who ran it, Josh and Tommy, were friends of the *Jase & PJ* show. They'd had Jase and PJ on before, and when they asked me to be a guest, I was so struck. Not necessarily because of who they were, but just because of what it meant for me. It felt like such an accomplishment to be asked to do something like that by people I didn't really know, and who wouldn't just be asking to make me feel good.

I did this podcast and had an absolute blast. And I mean, I really had SO much fun. After we were finished recording, we were all chatting outside and Josh and Tommy asked me if I'd be interested in starting my own podcast. Overwhelmed with excitement, we planned a meeting for a week later to have a brainstorm. The deal was going to be that they would cut it, edit it and produce it, while I would be the talent.

Me! Talent?! *Talent*. Talent!

We brainstormed and chatted and laughed and came up with some ideas about what it would look like, and that was the birth of my podcast, *One Trick Toni*.

I'd go to bed every night before a new episode came out thinking that I'd wake up with the podcast having gone viral overnight and I'd be the next *Shameless*. While that didn't happen, I did have lots of fun. I'd think about all the topics I wanted to cover and tell funny stories and have a great time, and it was great to have a little side project.

After a little while, though, because I was working very long hours in breakfast radio, I started to feel really burnt-out. I think it was a combination of overwork, itchy feet and wanting to move on to something a little different—and also feeling pretty defeated that my podcast hadn't blown up like I'd hoped. I decided that the podcast needed a bit of a hiatus so I could concentrate on my full-time job and figure out what I wanted to do next.

I told myself I'd never start another podcast again; too much work for no pay-off.

• • •

Let's rewind for a moment.

A few weeks before I called it quits on *One Trick Toni*, I'd been getting ready to go on summer holidays, when I found out I'd be working for an extra week on a summer breakfast radio show. You know how they do those special holiday shows when the actual hosts go on break and they get some celebrity fill-ins? That kind of thing. I was going to be working with this guy called Ryan Jon. (You're reading this book, right? I'm guessing you may have heard of him.)

I'd heard of Ryan before, being in the same radio circles, and we followed each other on Instagram, but I hadn't ever met him in person.

He walked into the room and I said, 'Hey, I'm Toni, so nice to meet you,' extending my hand for him to shake it. At the exact same time, he poked out his elbow for me to bump it, and my hand hit his elbow. It was very awkward and cute.

He said, 'I'm Ryan, how are you?'

And in the kerfuffle of awkward cuteness, I said, 'Oh, not great, I've got a pimple on my vagina and it's really uncomfortable.'

We became friends instantly.

After the holidays, I finished up *One Trick Toni* and was feeling incredibly uninspired and not sure what I wanted to do. Ryan and I were still working together, and anyone who has ever had the pleasure of knowing Ryan will know he's a pusher. And not in the way that Cady Heron claims Ms Norbury is a pusher in *Mean Girls*, but in this crazy, inspirational way.

It's almost frustrating how supportive Ryan is. And when I say 'almost', I mean it's really fucking frustrating because sometimes I just want to sit in my filth and do nothing, and he is always helping me up and pushing me up.

So after the podcast wound up, Ryan and I sat down together and he gave me some harsh truths. He began by asking me, 'What do you actually want to do? Where do you want to end up?'

'I want to be famous. I mean, I want to do what you do—make videos, be on the radio, make fun stuff on Instagram!'

'You know Instagram is free, right?' Ryan replied. 'Like, anyone can post? You could start doing that right now!'

See? FRUSTRATING!

'Well, yeah, I could do it right now. But, like . . . what if people don't like it and I look like a fuckhead?'

And he said something annoying along the lines of 'But what if people love it?', which just made me more frustrated. I was really, really scared of looking stupid. I didn't want to post something that people made fun of me for.

In a bitchy tone, I said, 'What if people think I'm just trying to get famous?'

And Ryan said, 'Toni, that's literally what you just told me you want to do.'

Yes, that's what I wanted to do, but I also didn't want to do it in case it didn't work and then I looked desperate, you know?

The conversation moved on and he asked me if I wanted to keep doing my podcast.

I said, 'I don't think a podcast will ever take off. Plus, they're just so much work for no return. It would be way easier for me to make three videos a week than one podcast episode.'

And, without realising, I'd given him the perfect ammunition. 'Well, then, why don't you make three videos a week?'

I didn't make three videos a week. I was too scared. So instead of making three videos a week, I made zero. Actually, in my defence, I did make a couple here and there, but nothing consistent.

Then I made this video of me in lockdown that went a bit viral. Em Rusciano shared it and my Instagram went CRAZY. Like, legitimately crazy. I got this taste for the satisfaction that came with something going well, and for the encouragement I got from Ryan. So I asked Ryan for some help making videos. I figured having someone else to bounce off, who could also help me get my confidence up, would help heaps.

It did.

Ryan and I went into the studio at KIIS, where he worked on a Saturday morning, armed with fifteen video ideas and ten different outfits, ready to make enough stuff to post over the next six weeks. We recorded everything and Ryan paid our mate Franco to cut up all the videos for us to post. We ended up spending the entire day together and had so much fun that we had dinner together that night too.

Then, something so amazing happened. The exact thing I'd hoped would happen with my podcast actually happened with our videos: they just went insane online. We'd post them and wake up to all of these views and new followers and it was AMAZING. I couldn't believe people liked what we were posting! Then we started getting all these comments from people asking, 'Where can I listen to the full podcast?'

I began replying to them, saying, 'We don't have a podcast, we just make videos!' but they didn't stop. Comment after comment after comment, asking where our podcast was.

The following weekend, Ryan and I were due to record a bunch more stuff together and we started talking about the comments people had left, saying they wanted to listen to our podcast. Immediately, we both agreed that it was too much work for probably no pay-off—we both had full-time jobs and other bits and pieces going on. It was just too much of a commitment. But we continued recording a bunch of videos together and had the most amazing fun.

A few weeks went past and we posted videos every day or two. Each video would do better than the last, and the comments asking for the podcast multiplied. I would look at my phone and cry because I couldn't believe people liked what we were creating. I couldn't believe there were people who wanted MORE of us! Something I'd always wanted and always dreamed of: it was almost too good.

Another recording day came around. Armed with ideas and ten different outfits, I put it all out there. 'Mate, these comments about our non-existent podcast won't let up,' I said. 'And I just wanna let you know, that if you're in, I'm in. Like, I'm all in. Let's fucking do this.'

I said everything I wanted to say in a way I never had before. I'd never had the confidence to be that vulnerable before, and it was such an empowering feeling.

Ryan looked at me and said, 'Yeah. I mean, yeah. Fuck yeah. Me too.'

And the *Toni and Ryan* podcast was born.

• • •

I went from replying to comments on TikTok with, 'We don't have a podcast, we just make videos!' to replying with, 'The *Toni and Ryan* podcast will be out August 23!'

Around the same time, Ryan was creating a sponsored ad for Instagram and asked me to be in it. It was so exciting, and we used the money we made from it to pay our mate Hayden Dib to take headshots and cover photos to use for the podcast.

When we launched, we started with three episodes a week, which of course is now five episodes a week. There was just the two of us in the Facebook group back then, but now there's an army of over 30,000 TARPers (*Toni and Ryan* podcast listeners) from all around the world. We also are now exclusive with Spotify—you know Spotify?! Spotify know who I am! It's such a huge dream come true.

And it started with me asking a brave question and asking for help from someone who believed in me. Someone who is now one of my best friends!

Something that started with the simplest, 'Fuck it, let's do it!' has turned into a job, and a career that is all of my dreams combined coming true every day.

I'm very #grateful.

I have never stolen someone else's butter from a workplace fridge

When I was a kid (and still now, actually), I was super dorky. I wasn't very confident in myself and it didn't take much to shake me or make me nervous. I've written about having anxiety through school, and this lack of confidence is just another manifestation of it, with the added pressure of being an adult and having to pay bills.

I also don't like inconveniencing anyone, which is a bit of a recipe for disaster. I'm not confident enough in my ability to back a decision I've made, and I don't like to annoy other people for advice or a vibe check. And I don't mean just on big decisions either, I mean anything.

Because my parents ran their own business, Mum wouldn't be able to just take days off here and there, so every time I had that funny, hot, sick feeling and Mum had to come and get me from the sick bay, I'd traipse into work with her and Dad.

I'd have to bring enough supplies to keep me busy—to avoid getting roped into doing work or answering phones—so I'd always have books and a Game Boy and all the other stuff kids used to like before they got iPads. It was the same during school holidays, before I was old and brave enough to stay home alone.

Then, when I finally was old enough to be home alone for school holidays and sick days, a whole new problem arose: what could I eat? A chubby little kid needs LIMITS. They need GUIDANCE. They need PARAMETERS.

So I'd call Mum.

In fact, every time I needed a little snacky or wanted to eat lunch, I'd call Mum and ask what was on offer. Sure, I could have just figured it out for myself, and I wish I could apologise to Mum now, but I can't, so hopefully she knows I just wanted to make sure I wasn't eating something I shouldn't. Imagine if I ate bread she was saving for lunches, or used up the last of the milk she needed for dinner that night? Terrifying!

I'd call and say, 'Hi Mum,' and she'd know straight away that I wanted to eat something and needed advice. And she'd sigh and say, 'Yep, Tone, that's fine, all good!' in a nice way while probably not feeling super happy about the interruption.

As I got older I started making more decisions, or at least planning out my meals better. If it was school holidays, for instance, to avoid needing to make a call, I'd make sure in advance that whatever I had my eye on was fair play. (Before we get into this next story, I'd like to very quickly clarify that nine times out of ten, Mum would say that whatever I wanted to eat was fine. So according to the law of averages, most things were all good, leaving me to use my best judgement.)

I was at home alone during the school holidays. I'd already eaten lunch and was sniffing around the kitchen for an afternoon snack. Right in the back of the freezer, I saw an old Sara Lee Chocolate Bavarian. It had been in there for ages and when I surveyed the box, I realised it hadn't even been opened.

A very quick tip from someone who is good at eating other people's food from the fridge: it's much easier to sneak a bit from food that's already been opened, because the owner of the food won't be surprised to find it open. Say you steal a line of chocolate from your housemate's open block, or a scrape of butter from the staffroom fridge at work, people probably won't notice that, because unless they're incredibly protective or you leave toast crumbs in the butter, they'll just assume it's as they left it. (I'll add here that there is a special place in hell for people who leave toast crumbs in butter or scrape their excess butter onto the side. Fuck you.) But if you open your housemate's block of chocolate, or steal the moment of clarity that peeling back the paper on a brand-new butter offers, they're going to fucking notice.

Back to the freezer. The Chocolate Bavarian wasn't open, but it had been there for quite some time, at least a month or two. After running a quick risk-versus-reward analysis in my brain, I decided that even though it was unopened, the amount of time it had been left in the freezer probably equalled it being a low-risk snack.

I carefully opened the cardboard box and slid out the foil pie dish. I then slowly uncrimped the edges of the foil to get to the Chocolate Bavarian. I'd never eaten a Bavarian before and didn't really know what a Bavarian was, actually, but figured it was kind of like ice-cream cake. I sliced myself a piece, carefully replaced the box in the back of the freezer—the open side facing the back—and sat down to enjoy the fruits of my labour.

It was fucking shit. Chocolate Bavarian is shit, and I won't hear another word about it. It's fucking awful. It's icy and disgusting and I hate it. It took a lot for me to not mindlessly snack, so it says something that I didn't even go back for seconds. The Chocolate Bavarian stayed in the back of the freezer, where it belonged.

Until about two months later.

• • •

I've mentioned birthdays were a big deal in the Lodge household, and that Mum would always organise the birthday dinner in the birthday person's preferred way.

But for this particular birthday dinner, Mum must have forgotten to organise a cake. Or maybe someone else was supposed to pick it up and they were running late and The Cheesecake Shop was closed. Or maybe someone had dropped the cake on the floor before it was time to eat it.

Thankfully, like me, my mum was very organised, and fucking hallelujah, right before we were supposed to have the cake, she remembered the birthday-saving Chocolate Bavarian in the back of the freezer.

'Oh, thank God I always have this for emergencies!' she whisper-celebrated to me in the kitchen.

It happened in slow motion. Mum reached into the back of the freezer as I realised what was about to happen. I felt myself turn white as a ghost. The noise of the party was suddenly torn from my ears, and all I could hear was the blood pumping through my brain at an escalated rate.

We couldn't sing 'Happy Birthday' over a cake with a slice taken out of it!

Mum opened the box and looked at me immediately (rude). The whisper-celebration turned very quickly to a whisper-yell. 'Toni Louise, did you eat this?!' Even though she and I knew full well it was a redundant question to ask of me, the family snack monster.

'No!' I lied. 'Oh my god, why, what's happened?!'

My mum knew I must be lying. This was the same woman who, knowing how deeply I loathed mint, had told me that her favourite biscuits and chocolate bars had mint in them so I wouldn't eat them out of the fridge. (It was only two years ago that Taubs bought himself a Chokito from the shops and offered me a bite, which I aggressively declined and got instantly fucked-off that he would even offer to me. 'You know I hate mint! Why would you offer me a Chokito?'

He laughed and it all added up in my brain. I wanted to be angry but smiled at the thought of my cheeky mum.)

Mum raised an eyebrow and I whisper-yelled, 'I didn't eat that!'

She thrust the almost full Chocolate Bavarian in my face and whisper-explained, 'Well, someone's eaten a slice of this. But who only eats one slice? What are we going to do?!'

I immediately reacted. 'Well, who the fuck would eat more than one slice? It's shit,' I said, not only revealing myself as the Bavarian thief, but making Mum annoyed that me ruining the birthday-saving cake wasn't even worth it.

My mum could get herself out of any situation. She made up a lie that she was going to give the dogs a slice of birthday cake before we sang 'Happy Birthday', and walked outside holding a plate with a tea towel over it—leaving [birthday person's name redacted] none the wiser about the cake fuck-up!

In all the hubbub, the Chocolate Bavarian had sat on the bench for around ten minutes, allowing it to defrost a little bit and actually leaving it the perfect temperature for consumption. (Even at the right temperature it was still shit, though.)

From then on, I knew that the backup cake was out of bounds.

I'll do that when I'm thinner

This is the most consistent lie I've told myself over the course of my life. This is also the one that makes me feel the most vulnerable, I think.

This is me taking off my baggy denim jacket and showing you that I'm not thin under here. It's me not wearing a jumper even though it's hot, it's me not just ordering the largest size I can find because I'm sure the clothes will look shit anyway, and it's better to have them look too big than go through the heartbreak of clothes coming and not fitting.

This lie is my version of 'I'll do that when my kids are older', or when it's not so hot, or when I make more money.

I've always been chubby.

When I was very little, I was fucking chubby and fucking cute. I had long hair and a fringe and was always wearing either a T-shirt and shorts with boots like my dad, or a dress with frilly socks and white leather sandals. I was absolutely gorgeous, and just as cheeky as I am now (with *slightly* less swearing). Isn't it odd that writing about myself as a child feels like I'm talking about someone else? I don't feel like I'm being vain, I'm just being kind to that little girl who loved playing with diggers and trucks as much as she did Barbies and her Baby Born doll called Kate.

When I started pre-primary, I loved school, and my teacher, Mrs Ancliffe, was so kind and loving. I never felt out of place, even though pre-primary was the first time I remember someone calling me fat.

This girl was tall and long and sporty—basically the complete opposite of me. At recess, while I was having my Uncle Tobys Roll-Up, she-who-will-not-be-named said, 'Toni, why is it you're so fat and I'm so skinny?'

I munched on that fucking roll-up and said, 'God just gave me more skin than you!'

To be honest I'm not really sure where the God angle came from. My family isn't religious whatsoever, but I didn't miss a beat.

As I got older, the kids around me became more aware that fat equalled bad, but they also gained a bit more tact. So instead of coming right out and telling me I was fat, they'd say it behind my back and make jokes about me.

I remember going to the shops with a bunch of girlfriends (hanging out at the shops was cool then) and running into another group of friends they had from another school. The next day—

I was told—the other group of girls asked my own friends, 'Who was that fat friend with you?' before laughing at my expense.

It got harder as my friends started kissing boys, because I figured no one would ever want to smooch me. Why would they? I hated myself, so why would anyone else want to smooch up on me?

I was the girl dancing alone at parties and clubs while my much hotter friends danced with people they fancied who paid for their drinks at the bar.

When I did lose weight, people would say things like, 'You look so much better!' and 'Wow, you are looking so *healthy*!' which is just the most fucking shitty thing you can say. Cut the shit and say, 'Remember when you looked fat and awful and we were afraid to be seen with you? Thank God that isn't the case now!'

But I've always been chubby. I've fluctuated from fat to chubby to slim and back again for my whole life. The way I've been treated by others has changed with every fluctuation, and the way I treat myself has changed too.

At my thinnest, I knew I deserved love and opportunities and I let myself enjoy life. At my biggest sizes, I've been embarrassed, I've struggled letting other people see my body and I've avoided mirrors.

What this boils down to is that, for most of my life, I thought that when I was thin, I'd be happy. And that when I was happy, I'd be confident. But I have managed to find happiness and confidence outside of that. Realising this has changed me.

So here I would like to write a list of things I'd always told myself I'd do when I was thinner—to immortalise a bucket list of things that are absolutely not affected by my body shape or weight.

Some of these have already actually been ticked off—there is something quite exhilarating about telling yourself to get fucked and just living your best life. Remove the caveats you've placed on your enjoyment and your life! Take off your version of your baggy denim jacket, write out your version of this list, and *do the fuck out of it.*

☑ **Travel**

I'd see girls travelling around the world, and diving off boats into blue oceans and backpacking with confidence, and always told myself I'd 'be able to' do that when I was thin. Actually, I can do it whenever the fuck I want. Not yet ticked off—but it will be.

☑ **Post funny videos on Instagram**

This one's been ticked off, obviously. I was very scared to post videos on Instagram and TikTok. I knew all of the comments would say I was fat instead of saying I was funny. But I surprised myself, and thankfully my hair was so shit that people bullied me for that instead! I've also had to constantly remind myself that thousands of positive comments are more important than one bad one.

☑ **Buy nice clothes that fit my body**

This one's a work in progress. I feel like I've always had the attitude of 'I can't wait to fit into that!' when the truth is that my body isn't wrong; it's the clothes. I only hope that even more brands make larger sizes a bit more accessible.

☑ **Move my body in ways I enjoy, like dancing and swimming**

I remember telling myself, 'I'll be able to start swimming for fitness once I'm thinner!' Girl, what? I love to swim. I've always been a strong swimmer. So now I just jump in the fucking pool and go for it. TICK!

☑ **Get Invisalign**

I thought I needed to wait until I was thin to have a beautiful smile I was proud of. Now look at me! I never shut my mouth!

☑ **Join the gym**

Similar to above. I have decided I don't need to be thinner before I go to the gym.

☑ **Write more**

You're looking at it! Tick!

☑ **Get my dream job**

Once again, you're looking at it! Tick, tick!

☑ **Find a perfect life partner**

We're on a roll here—tick times 100!

☑ **Be on a billboard**

I told my mum I'd be on a billboard one day—who knows, maybe! But it's not going to happen because of my body shape. It's gonna be because I'm doing the fuck out of everything else I love.

☑ **Have confidence**

I'm happy to half tick this one off. I'm getting there. I love my life and I'm so proud of how far I've come. Full tick coming soon.

☑ **Enjoy food without feeling self-conscious**

Another work in progress. I think you could also file this one under 'not giving a fuck what other people think'.

☑ **Stop getting dressed up to go to the shops or run an errand because I'm afraid of looking sloppy instead of cute and underdone**

I'm so busy these days that I've definitely gone to the shops in tracksuit pants and been recognised. The world did *not* explode!

☑ **Be myself**

Fucking TICK. Funny, chubby and just *me*.

Things keeping me up at night

◎ How come every episode of the TV show *House* has an episode description? Every episode starts with someone falling ill unexpectedly, and then House and his team fix it, but then another symptom crops up that they weren't antici-pating, only for House to have an epiphany and solve it simply in the end. Literally all of the synopses could be: 'Person falls ill. House's diagnostic team work to solve it.'

◎ Fuck, I'm writing a book. I need to write 20,000 more words. What the fuck am I going to write about? Am I interesting enough for a book?

◎ What's that song that goes, 'da da dada da da da dadadada'? I'll have to google that in the morning.

◎ What would I do if Taubs died? Will the excitement of our future—getting married or buying a house or him offering me a coffee every morning—be taken away too soon?

◎ Does having something so fantastic that I'm so terrified to lose just make it more special?

◎ Should I stop wasting time on these questions and just go and smooch my handsome boyfriend before it's too late? I guess I pick that one.

◎ Are all of the doors locked? I better get up and check.

◎ How come I'd sacrifice my own time for work without a second thought, but never for myself? Why don't I just wake up early to exercise or meditate when I know it'll make my day so much better? If I had to wake up at 4 a.m. for work, I'd do it without question (and I have), but the thought of waking up half an hour earlier to go for a walk is like torture. Why don't I value my own health and time more?

◎ I wish I didn't fall asleep on the couch this afternoon; I'll never sleep tonight now.

◎ Is the oven still on? I better go check. And the hair straightener.

◎ Ahhh, why am I not asleep yet?!

◎ Should I cut my hair short? Short hair is so cool, but long hair takes so long to get to a good spot. Is my face too chubby for short hair? Am I hiding behind a security blanket of long hair? Do I need to discuss this with my therapist?

◎ Stop thinking about Taubs dying!

◎ Fuck, I have to pay that hot water bill.

I hate children

When I was a kid, my mum cut this article she loved out of the newspaper, and it lived on the fridge. It was there after she died, it was there when I moved out, it's probably still there now. It was a list of milestones of life. I remember not really understanding it, to be honest, but it's stuck with me for all these years.

There were obvious things, like earning your first pay cheque and buying a house—but there was another, more peculiar one, which was 'holidaying alone, and loving it', which really offended me. Why would my mum want to holiday without ME?

Then last year, I stayed at a winery by myself for three days and it was absolute bliss. I watched TV, ate, had a massage and a facial, took myself out for dinner and read my book, and had seven thousand baths. Honestly, could not recommend it more.

Also on the list of milestones was becoming a parent.

• • •

My mum LOVED being a mum. She adored looking after all of us, hearing our stories and playing with us. She just loved being loved. She loved being needed and it made her feel so special to be gifted homemade cards and macaroni jewellery and all the other shit we subject our parents to. She also had a career and seemed to be fulfilled. And because of how much she loved being a mum, it made us kids love being part of such a big family, and I always dreamed of that for myself.

As a kid, there are all these things that you assume are going to be in your life, so looking at this list of life milestones on the fridge, I was like okay, these are the points I'll hit in my journey and then that's it. Not that you can't deviate from that, but why would you want to? This journey is so perfect and straightforward! You finish school, go to uni, start a job you'll have for the rest of your life, get married at 22, buy a house, have a baby at 24 and live happily ever after.

So, like lots of girls, I assumed growing up that I would be a mum. When I was little, my favourite toy was this baby dolly who I cleverly named Baby. I loved her, and she went every-where with me, including to make mud pies in the backyard, which Mum came out to see me shoving into Baby's mouth. This required immediate toy surgery, but Mum got her cleaned up. After carrying Baby around for a few years, I was desperate for an upgrade.

The thing I wanted more than ANYTHING was a Baby Born. You'll remember the one, and if you don't, google it. They weren't your average, run-of-the-mill baby dollies. They could cry and wee and each one was like a perfect replica of an actual baby.

I finally got one for my fifth birthday, and named her Kate. Kate came everywhere with me. I had a baby carrier and even a legit, name-brand Baby Born stroller that I forced Mum to let me take to the shops so I could roll Kate around with us.

I also had an early insight into parenting when Tamagotchis, a type of digital pet, became popular. I took my role and responsibility as a digital pet parent very seriously and the little guy was so well cared for. I'd erase his little digital poos and give him tiny doses of digital medicine when he had a skull-and-crossbones above his head. I used to take him to school and pop him under my tray so I could give him food and water when he needed it without my teacher noticing.

When we had our sports carnival, I taught Mum how to look after my Tamagotchi for the day. She took her role of digital pet grandma very seriously too. For the week leading up to the carnival, whenever a symbol came up, I'd test Mum on how she would handle the problem, and she always passed with flying colours.

I was 11 when my nephew Tyler was born. I was really scared to go from being the baby of the family to having someone else who was younger, but the moment I met him, I was smitten, and have adored him more and more every day since I first saw that little smile on the day he was born. Because we were almost closer in age than I was with my actual siblings, we developed a really close, special relationship and I loved hanging out with and babysitting him with Mum, so much so that we would take him off my brother and sister-in-law at any opportunity we got.

Tyler couldn't say my name when he was little, so I have been known as Totti since then, and I love it. He's now a *proper* teenager, who on FaceTime the other day said, 'I better be in your book,' but won't let me follow him on Instagram. I was never that angsty.

When my sister-in-law got pregnant again, with my niece Ashlee, I was scared to have another baby in the family. I remember panicking to Mum and Libby, saying that I didn't have enough love inside me for another little baby. I loved Tyler more than ANYTHING, how could I love another tiny babe? But Ashlee stole my heart the second I saw her and I love her to death.

This meant that when Libby had her children, Lawson and Wes, and when Hayley and her wife had a baby, I knew exactly what to expect. I got to snuggle them and sniff them and love them to death . . . but I also got to hand them back. I could babysit and hold babies whenever their mum or dad needed a break, and I could forever be the fun aunt.

It was the same when my friends started having babies. I would get to snuggle them and smooch them and spoil them, but unlike my friends, I could also sleep in on a Saturday morning instead of going to footy practice. I didn't have to juggle my life and career with Taubs' life and career, and add a baby's life into the mix. Of course, there are people who have a baby and a career, and people who have one or the other, or a combination of those two things and more! And I take my hat off to parents—I really do.

But isn't it weird that having a baby is the default journey?

We live in a time where things have never been more expensive, there's never been more people (have you been on a train lately?) and we've never had more freedom. We're breaking away from the traditions that our parents' generation had thrust onto them. Like, we live with our partners before we get married, we change careers and go to uni later in life, we take time off to avoid burnout—all the things they never did. So, why would having someone dependent on me for eighteen years still be the default?!

The week Taubs and I moved in together, we had a really serious conversation. Having children came up and I remember saying, 'That's just not for me.' I immediately realised how intense a thing that was to say. It just came to me in that moment! I don't think I'd ever explored the option to not have children before that moment, but it was exactly how I felt.

We had a long talk about it, which ended with me saying, 'I love kids, but I just don't think I'll ever want kids. If that's a deal-breaker then I don't know if we have a future.'

First of all, holllllly fuck, Toni! Moving house is such intense admin, as if we couldn't have had that conversation before ferrying all of our things into a house where both our names were on the lease?

Taubs responded the best way someone could. 'I love kids, too, but I'd rather have you than a child.'

And that's the way it's stayed ever since.

• • •

I was really proud of myself for having the guts to say that, and to go against the grain of a society that automatically assumes you'll be having children. Children are a huge commitment and I wanted to concentrate on my career and not give myself any time limits or set any expectations that I might not be able to meet.

But it wasn't until a bit later that the full weight of the expectation that I would have children seemed to hit me. I got older and people started asking when Taubs and I would get married or when we would have children. I even had someone say to me once that it was good that I was moving around for my job early in life, to get it out of my system before I was tied down with a baby.

I've also had people say to me that my choice is feminism gone wrong and it's 'just a phase that I'll get over'. I've had someone say to me, 'You'll know what it's like when you're a mum!', to which I've responded that I don't want children right now, and they've then said, 'But you'd be such a good mum!'

First of all, you shouldn't do something like that just because you might be good at it. Second, I don't think I would be! I could love a baby like CRAZY, but I'm also a major stress-head and very overbearing. I'm not very patient and I worry about too many things. I also like sleeping in on a Saturday and my car not having crumbs in it unless they're from me eating a Subway cookie on the go.

Another 'reason' to have children that I've been told is: 'Don't you want someone to look after you when you're old?! You don't want to be lonely!'

I really don't think that is a good reason to have children. I'm not selfish for not wanting children; the selfish choice here for me would be to have them just so it's easier for me in the future.

Why do I have to justify this to anyone anyway? Again, how is me not wanting to commit to raising and supporting someone for eighteen years the *odd choice*?

I've also had someone tell me (without the context of knowing I didn't want children) that women (not people, *women!*) who don't want children 'hate kids and hate women who have them'.

This is entirely untrue for me. I LOVE babies. I love mums! I love people who decide to have children! I love my nieces and nephews, I love my friends' kids, I have friends who see children in their futures and I can't WAIT to snuggle those little babes! And Taubs is the same. Loves to snuggle babies and sniff their soft little heads. It's just not for us, and that's okay.

The same way it's okay if we change our minds! If in the future, we realise we have more money than we thought we would or our priorities change or we feel like something is missing from our lives—we are allowed to change our minds. It's our life, and we'll decide what we want to do in our own time and without anyone else's opinion in mind.

This side of the conversation is rarely shown. Whenever I talk about it openly, I get so many messages from people who mirror my sentiment and have had very little support from their family in their choice. I also get many messages from people with fertility problems, who are hearing the same things as me, even though it's not their choice to be child-free.

There's just never a good reason to ask someone this shit. Fuck off and think about your own life, I reckon.

Reasons the world is against me— I can't trust my family, friends or boyfriend

Throughout my life, as you know by now, I haven't ever had a 'best friend'. You know how some people have that special first person who, regardless of what is happening, knows every detail of your life and is the one you call with good news and bad news? The one you call and say, 'You know that café I go to all the time? They don't do that chicken sandwich anymore! Maybe I'll try that other one Celeste posted about on her Instagram story the other day. Did you see she got engaged? By the way, I got my period. Anyway, call me back later.' Or whatever best friends do.

I have, and have had, plenty of fantastic friends, but I've always been a bit of a floater. I've got lots of best friends, but they all have other best friends, too. So, all of the great friends I have *already* have the other person they call about the chicken sandwich and Celeste being engaged.

Mindy Kaling once explained that a best friend isn't a person, it's a tier. And I think I'm a really good example of that.

I don't really know how I feel about this, to be honest. I guess Taubs is my best friend? He's the person I call with good news, bad news and chicken sandwich news—but is that lame? I feel like everyone posts on Instagram when they get engaged that they get to 'marry their best friend', but you KNOW there's a *real* best friend on the sidelines teaching them to use a hairdryer and convincing them to try a new brand of underwear that they saw on Instagram.

For argument's sake, let's say Taubs is my best friend. Before that though, my mum was probably my best friend. She was the person I told everything to and I would float ideas about outfits and boys and whatever else with her. She was definitely my chicken sandwich phone call.

Then I have many other people sitting on what we'll now refer to as my 'best friend tier'.

Étain, who I've been BFFs with since we were at uni—a very cool artist who currently has a bleached and shaved head. As stated, she is incredibly cool and she doesn't give a fuck what anyone thinks. She is also someone who, when I went to her mum and dad's house for the first time, said, 'I made the park bench we're sitting on.' She does many other random, fantastic things.

There's Jane, who I worked with in radio, who lives in the most delicious townhouse in a chic area of South Melbourne, which for anyone not in Melbourne, is a very cool spot where no one would be caught dead without a takeaway coffee and a dog on a Country Road lead—including Jane. Very fashionable and very fun and never one to pay full price for clothes, Jane always texts something lovely on hard days to remind me she loves me.

Then there's the second love of my life, Lain, who will definitely be forced into helping me wee in my wedding dress one day. As mentioned, she looks exactly like Blake Lively and it makes me sick. Lain is very kind and is always the first to include people so they don't feel left out—and always very keen on learning a new dance or choreographing for others at any opportunity.

But even though all of these people are fantastic, I can't trust any of them.

As you would also know by now, for a long time I wanted to be famous. I'd post stupid videos expecting overnight virality and success, and they didn't come. But then, one day, they did! I posted this video saying how much I hated that curly font you can use on a Samsung phone, and it went fucking crazy. I think it ended up landing somewhere around a million views in only a couple of days, and getting thousands and thousands of comments. So many comments in agreeance, and lots of comments saying that the alternative was using an iPhone, and iPhones are shit. (Just as a side note, the alternative to using the curly font on a Samsung phone is actually NOT an iPhone—it's just not using that stupid fucking font. This sounds like an overreaction but sorry, the font is fucking atrocious and I hate it so much.)

The other brand of comments on this video had nothing to do with the iPhone vs Samsung debate. They were telling me how SHIT MY HAIR WAS.

For a very long time—and by long time, I mean on and off for ten years—I styled my hair the same way: a short front fringe. A micro fringe, I think is what they're called. The look is similar to Bettie Page's, and affectionately known as Bettie Bangs.

For a full decade, at no point did a friend, family member or boyfriend tell me that my hair was shit and awful. No, I had to find out from the INTERNET, which is just the worst place to discover something negative.

I looked through the comments (which is breaking the one rule of being on the internet: don't read the comments) and was in disbelief. First of all, I was shocked people weren't commenting on me being fat. I'd prepared myself for that, but not THIS!

Second, I couldn't believe people were making fun of this awesome and cool fringe I'd been committed to for all of this time. Isn't that just so awful? But as I continued to scroll through those comments, I thought that maybe they had a point. This many people couldn't be wrong.

So I decided to ask the local population—all the lovely and delightful ladies in my life listed above, the girls at work, Taubs and basically anyone else who'd listen.

'People on this video are saying my hair is so shit! I had no idea it was that bad! Is it that bad?!'

To which every single person I asked said, 'Oh my God, absolutely not! Your fringe is so fucking cute! It's so *you*, Toni!' in that high-pitched lying voice you use when you've been bitching about how a waiter got your order wrong, and then the very same waiter comes over and asks how everything is and you go, 'Oh my GOD everything is perfect! I've never eaten a better chicken satay!' even though you ordered the steak and are suffering through mild anaphylaxis due to the peanut allergy you warned them about.

I realised that there was only one option: fuck the fringe completely off. SEE YA LATER FRINGE, THANKS FOR NOTHING.

A very difficult three months ensued, of braiding my fringe out of the way and begging hairdressers to fix it. Since then, I have had a long fringe and I will never cut it in again, because my real friends—STRANGERS ON THE INTERNET—told me the truth.

I'm not afraid of the thing that killed my mum

Not long after Ryan and I started the podcast, my Instagram began to blow up a bit with people loving the videos and enjoying the podcast. I started to not be able to keep up with messages. As soon as I would clear out my inbox, it would fill up again. It was the craziest feeling—something I'd always wanted to happen was happening so quickly and I was super grateful for it, and still am! I adore it so much. That's the really special thing about Instagram and our Facebook group, we get to talk to so many people and it's fucking awesome.

One of the things I have loved about the podcast and everything that's come with it has been sharing my stupid stories and dumb questions with people from all over the world. I mean, from getting catfished by a girl in America who I mistook for Robert Pattinson to the many times I've shit myself around the world—I've done it all. There's really not much I'm afraid to share!

So when I noticed a rash on my nipple in late 2021, I shared it.

Off the cuff, I mentioned something about having a cracked and super itchy nipple, and asked anyone who had breastfed or experienced something similar to what I was going through to slide into my DMs and let me know what had helped them.

Expecting people to tell me the name of some wonder balm, instead I received hundreds of messages along the lines of: 'Toni. This is not funny, you need to go to the doctor,' and 'I had that, and I've just finished going through chemo.'

I didn't know this, but apparently, any change in your nipples or breasts can be the beginning of Paget's disease, which is usually a sign of breast cancer. I googled the condition to within an inch of its life, and every photo, example or description of Paget's disease looked and sounded exactly like my nipple. There was almost no denying that it was exactly what I had.

Even though I'd decided there was no way that I could have breast cancer, I booked an appointment with my GP, Tom, to be safe. He's a great doctor who I've been seeing for years since moving to Melbourne, and he's someone who knows I'm prone to overthinking things. Assuming that I was going to walk in there and he was going to tell me I was fine and not to worry, I figured the appointment would clear my mind and set me at ease.

I walked in expecting to be told it was okay, in other words. But after having a look, Tom seemed to think it could be something more sinister, and I walked out with referrals for breast ultrasounds and mammograms.

It was right before Christmas and I wasn't able to get an appointment anywhere until after the holidays, so I spent my holiday break worrying over what was wrong. I told myself to calm down, but it was playing on my mind so much. Did I actually have cancer? Was I going to die? Would I have to go through chemo? All I wanted to do was talk to my mum and have her tell me it was going to be okay.

I was so scared of having cancer. So scared of the thought of dying from this same thing that had taken my lovely, perfect mum away from me.

After the Christmas break was over, I was finally able to have my appointments and then go back to my GP to review everything. My nipple was looking worse, and I was getting really worried. Nothing was clear and Tom wasn't sure, so I ended up having an emergency appointment with the celebrity breast cancer doctor Chantel Thornton.

Normally, it takes a few months to get an appointment with Dr Chantel, but I had one within half an hour. As exciting as it was to meet the queen of breasts, I was terrified. It was a bad sign that I had to meet her—and an even worse sign that I was able to see her at such short notice.

I went straight over to her practice and waited on the bench outside, worrying myself sick. After what felt like an eternity I was called into Dr Chantel's office. She was the kindest person I'd ever met, so lovely and so efficient. She made me feel at ease and asked me a lot of questions about my life and my boobies.

She took a look at all of my scans and then examined me. Deciding she needed some more clarity, she then booked me in for another breast ultrasound and mammogram, and asked, 'How are you with pain?'

I'm pretty good with pain, to be quite honest. I have a reasonably high pain threshold and not a lot really fazes me, but I do get anxious before a procedure.

'Yeah, pretty good . . . why's that?'

'We're going to need to take a punch biopsy right now and send it away for testing,' she said. 'And it's going to hurt.'

Hanging on to her nurse Victoria's hand for dear life, scared stupid that I was about to find out I had cancer, stressed about the pain and thankful for health insurance, I lived through the biopsy and booked in to see Dr Chantel three days later to get my results.

Three days.

I got home to Taubs and called Jamie. I felt strangely calm, being in this very odd place where I was really scared, but had to be patient. I didn't want to freak Taubs out and I didn't want to worry Jamie, but I didn't know what else I could do. I tried to keep life as normal as possible, but something like waiting on test results makes time move so much more slowly. My face was still happy and my mouth was saying 'let's just see what happens!', but my brain was scrambled like eggs at a buffet.

Thankfully, after three long days, I was very lucky to find out that I was negative for Paget's disease and all clear for breast cancer.

I couldn't believe it. A month's worth of worrying, all leading up to this moment of Dr Chantel telling me I was clear.

As I waited in reception to pay for my appointment, I was in a daze. I stumbled out of the practice and tripped down the steps and got in my car. Before driving home, I texted Jamie: 'I don't have cancer!!!!!!!!!!!!!!!!'

I started driving. My phone rang through the Bluetooth and I answered.

Jamie yelled, 'WHAT DID I JUST READ? ARE YOU SURE?!'

And I screamed, 'I don't have cancer!' before pulling over one metre from where I'd just been parked and bawling my eyes out on the phone to my brother for five full minutes. Every little tear that I hadn't let escape while I was waiting for my appointments, waiting for a verdict, waiting to know what I should do.

Jamie conferenced in his wife and we all just cried on our three-way phone call. I was sitting in the car on the side of the road for about half an hour before realising I had to get home and celebrate with Taubs.

• • •

I thought facing the thing that took my mum away from me would be hard, but being clear of it was really conflicting. On the one hand, I was so lucky and grateful to have the all-clear. But it made me wish so bad that my mum had been that lucky too.

I'm excited about everything

There's no right way to grieve. There's no right way to heal, there's no right way to laugh or cry or look after yourself. You have to listen to yourself and let your body and surroundings tell you, right?

It's a bit like when you get your driver's licence. You know the right things to do, and you know on paper how things should sound or feel. You know you're supposed to look in your rear-view mirror every six to eight seconds, but you don't really know *what* you're looking for.

Look, I failed my practical driving test like five times, so maybe this was just me. But it was like I knew what to do, but I didn't know why. I knew what could go wrong but I didn't really know how to react if it did.

When my mum died, I didn't really know what to do, and I wasn't old enough to know myself yet. I didn't trust myself, I was judging myself really harshly about how I was behaving and I didn't want my family to worry about me.

Relearning life without my mum felt like this HUGE task, and if I'd failed my driving test five times, how the fuck could I handle this?

• • •

After Mum died, I deferred my uni course to the following year and, to keep myself busy, I joined the gym. I went to the gym every single morning, then worked at Coles during the day and on weekends. I didn't do a lot else. I don't think I did all that much in the way of healing or dealing with the whole dead mum situation at all, but I kept myself busy with a bunch of random things.

On the one-year anniversary of Mum dying, it was (obviously) really sad. I skipped uni for the day and visited her grave with my family, and thought to myself, 'Well that's the end of that chapter.'

No longer had my mum 'recently died', because it had been a whole year. It was no longer a shock, I was no longer going to bump into people who didn't know, and it was no longer a fresh wound. It was like the calendar ticking over to that day meant I had to dust my hands of my grief and move along.

So, I did what any twenty-year-old would do, and posted on Instagram.

It's actually still there, the post I made a couple of days after the one-year anniversary, so if you scroll allllllllll the way back through my many selfies and travel snaps and food photos to 12 September 2014, you'll see a photo of my mum, Libby and me, and a standing quote card that says: Today I am excited about everything.

I have captioned the post by saying, 'A year ago today, my life was in pieces. But today, I am excited about everything. Thank you for everything you gave me. Love you, miss you.'

I felt the need to flick the switch on my grief and shut the door. I really and truly believed with all of my soul that that was it. Not because I wasn't sad or because I was used to it or over it or anything like that. But in the same way we say, 'The diet starts Monday!' or 'I'll join the gym on 1 January', the anniversary felt like a natural end to this period and I desperately wanted it to all be over.

Otherwise, what? Wait until the following anniversary? Another YEAR of GRIEF?

Spoiler alert: it wasn't over.

The door was still open, the light was still on, the chapter wasn't closed and it was a fresh wound. It was like a cut on your finger that constantly reopens and continues to sting.

To be honest, that second year was one of the hardest. In fact, every year I would reach the next anniversary and think, 'This one's the year! It won't hurt anymore!' But it still did.

I feel really naive for having thought that.

Now, I don't miss her any less or love her any less, and it doesn't hurt any less, but I've gotten used to it. I know the ways I can move my finger without the cut opening up. Then sometimes the cut opens up, but it doesn't make me sad anymore, or I can push through the pain because now I know how to express my feelings or use a band-aid when it's too much.

One of the biggest shocks I've had since losing my mum was the sudden realisation that I needed to fill that love void. All of a sudden, my life was really different and there was a heap of love missing. Not because she didn't love me anymore, but because the constant pushes of support and gushes of pride had disappeared. My cheerleader was gone—and I realised that the support and pride I needed now had to come from me.

I had to take the love that she'd left behind for me and give it to myself. It was like learning to love myself: I already had all of the tools, I just needed to learn to self-medicate—to repurpose it.

That's been the toughest part, but also the most rewarding.

I've never shat myself in the street

This lie may be reminiscent of that scene from *Bridesmaids*, which is one of the best movies maybe ever made. It is hilarious and so fun, and it reignited the world's passion for the song 'Hold On' by Wilson Phillips, which is a true act of public service, if you ask me. We can all do with a little more of that song in our lives.

That aside, I feel like it would be remiss of me not to discuss the embarrassing things that have happened to me—things that, though they're funny to look back on, were not funny at the time. When I was planning to write this book, I tried to group all of my experiences and think about how they'd all fit together. At that point, I realised I had three separate stories about shitting myself in public. Now, most people would run from that. They'd shy away from the fact that they'd shit themselves in public more than once, and that they were above the age of three, and that each incident had occurred in the middle of a street.

But here we are.

• • •

The earliest instance of me shitting myself in public (when out of nappies) happened when I was walking home from school one day.

I was in Year 6, so probably around eleven years old. I grew up in the hills of Perth, in a small suburb called Roleystone. Pretty much everyone knew everyone, and we'd all gone through primary school together, so everyone's mum knew everyone's mum. It was the kind of place where, when you went to the shops after school, it would take twenty minutes to buy milk because you'd bump into several people your mum knew and they'd have a chinwag.

I'd walk to and from school most days, along with a massive horde of other kids, arriving or leaving at the same time because we all lived so close. There was a main road, Raeburn Road, where you'd just see every kid in Roleystone walking in the same direction. It was also a really chill school, and we just had to wear a light blue polo shirt, with anything else on the bottom as long as it was navy blue.

This one day in particular, I was wearing dark blue tracksuit pants from Supré, which was this iconic cool girl shop. On this afternoon, after the bell rang, I joined the mass exodus of kids leaving school on foot. I had a friend in tow, who was going to walk home with me to hang out and play PlayStation or whatever.

We were walking towards my house, along with 100 other kids, when I realised my tummy was a bit sore and I didn't feel too well. But this unnamed friend and I kept walking and chatting to each other and to the other kids on the road.

Very quickly, though, I understood that I was in a bit of trouble poo wise and, still being a fifteen-minute walk away from my house, it started to scare me. My demeanour must have completely changed, but this unnamed friend didn't let on that she'd realised something was wrong.

So we kept walking with the mass of other kids, who all began to peel off towards their own homes. As they turned off the road, we continued walking straight, and I started to feel like I just couldn't hold it in anymore.

We picked up the pace and I tried to play it cool by chatting and laughing and walking, but I was right: I couldn't hold it in anymore.

I pooed. In the street.

Still walking, still talking, but also pooing.

Then I had to walk the rest of the way home with poo in my knickers without dying of embarrassment. We finally got home and I rushed past Mum in the kitchen, excusing myself to go to her ensuite to try to sort myself out. I cleaned myself up but quickly realised I didn't have any spare knickers or pants to change into.

I poked my head around the wall to see the unnamed friend sitting on the couch, watching *Judge Judy* and making small talk with my mum—right where I needed to walk past to get some clean knickers.

I managed to grab Mum's attention and signalled her to distract the unnamed friend so I could prance through the house with only my school polo on to get some clean knickers and pants (and to throw my old ones out on the way through).

I walked out three minutes later in different pants, but still wearing my school polo shirt, and played it cool. I don't think the unnamed friend bought it, but she NEVER brought it up and neither did I.

• • •

The second story I'll share actually happened not long after the first one. We were on holidays in Broome and it was just Mum, Dad and me. My siblings must have been busy with work or uni at the time, so the three of us had ventured up alone.

As I've mentioned, we'd stay in a caravan park, sleeping in a camper trailer which, obviously, didn't have a toilet. You would do all bathroom things in the ablution block in the centre of the park. We had been there for a couple of days and were having so much fun, eating, exploring and surfing.

Then, one afternoon, after being out all day, I started feeling really faint. Mum assumed I had just been in the sun too long, so she set me up to lay down with the fan on me and some cold water. She went off to have a shower while Dad sat outside, talking on the phone to one of my sisters.

Lying inside in absolute agony, I decided that maybe I needed something to eat or some fresh air, so I hopped up and walked out of the tent, looked at my dad and just threw up on the spot.

Obviously alarmed, he jumped up and grabbed me so I didn't fall down. I started crying because I felt so sick, and was obviously super embarrassed that I'd just thrown up. Dad made a bit of a face and I said, 'Dad, don't, I know it's disgusting, I'm so sorry!'

And he said, 'That's okay, just don't sit down.'

I hadn't even realised, but the sheer force I'd exerted in throwing up had actually made me poo myself at the same time.

I'm not sure if this goes for all dads, but mine wasn't super prepared or well equipped to deal with this, but I obviously couldn't walk all the way to the ablution block covered in my own vomit and diarrhoea. So he came up with a plan.

As Mum was walking back from her shower, all clean and beautiful, all she saw was us standing around the side of our campsite, away from everyone, Dad with a big bucket of (freezing cold) water in one hand, holding my pants away from my body with the other hand, ready to tip the bucket of (freezing fucking cold) water down my pants to 'flush it out'.

Mum rushed over, probably ready to share her own, more sophisticated idea about how to handle this *shituation*, but it was too late. Dad was pouring.

It was absolutely not a good plan of attack, and I don't know why we thought it was the best option, because now not only did I feel poorly, I was also soaking wet.

• • •

'But Toni, that's not you shitting in the street? These are supposed to be stories of you shitting in the street, aren't they?' I hear you ask. Please be patient.

• • •

We went to the doctors' the next day. They told me I had gastro and it would clear up in the next day or two, I just needed to drink heaps of Hydralyte and Gatorade and eat super plain food. So for the next couple of days of our delish sunny holiday, I was on strict bed rest inside the tent while trying to not throw up and poo myself every five minutes.

Thankfully, after a couple of days, it cleared up and I felt way better and was ready to try to enjoy the last week of our holiday.

One of our favourite things to do in Broome was to have lunch at the Roebuck Bay Hotel, affectionately known as The Roey, which sits on the main drag. Mum and Dad would always get chilli garlic prawns, and I'd always get a chicken parmigiana.

We decided to break my fast, in which I'd only eaten salty crackers with nothing on them, with my favourite holiday meal. I was so fucking excited to eat something and get some sun.

We had the yummiest meal and I was so glad to be feeling better. We also bumped into a guy my dad had done some business with, and he and his wife joined us.

When we finished up, we all walked back down the street towards the car. And then, as we were passing the Sun Pictures outdoor movie theatre on the main street of Broome, I realised that I definitely wasn't better and wished I'd never eaten the chicken parmigiana—and I threw the whole thing up.

In front of Mum, Dad, Dad's business friend and his wife, and every tourist in Broome, I threw up and pooed in my Roxy denim shorts.

You might be thinking, 'Wow, Toni, please stop now.'

But I will not. We're almost there.

• • •

This is a story which, if you've listened to my podcasts in the past, you may be familiar with, but here it is again. It really rounds out the trifecta of me shitting in the street.

It was about a week before my 21st birthday. Taubs and I had been sleeping together for ages, but we'd only been boyfriend and girlfriend officially for about six weeks. I was studying at uni and working at Coles on the weekends. I was still living at home with my dad, but he was working away for a couple of weeks, so I was there alone.

Like any kid who has the house to themselves while their parent is away, I ate shitty food for every meal. On the menu for this particular fancy Friday night was a frozen pizza and crispy M&Ms. I ate the pizza and got halfway through a bag of the M&Ms before falling asleep.

I woke up on Saturday morning, ready to work a full day in the Coles deli, and decided to fuel my body with the rest of the bag of crispy M&Ms. I basically inhaled those bad boys while rushing around, getting ready to leave for work.

I arrived at the deli, started to feel super queasy and managed to run all the way upstairs to the staff bathroom before throwing up VIOLENTLY in the toilet. All I could taste was artificial sweetener, and all I could see was the blue dye from those barely digested M&Ms.

Chalking it up to definitely having just eaten a bag of chocolate for breakfast, I figured I was fine to start my shift. But then, NOPE! I'M GOING TO THROW UP AGAIN.

I called the store from the floor of the toilet and told my team in the deli that I must have gastro and there was no way I should be handling food. I was going to go home as soon as I could scoop myself up off the floor.

I stayed in there for a while. I just could NOT stop throwing up. It was like a clown car—when I decided it was impossible for anything else to come out, it would just keep pouring out.

Finally, I stopped throwing up for long enough to brave the fifteen-minute drive home. I made it home (Lord knows how) and jumped into the shower to try to freshen myself up. I called Taubs from the floor of the bathroom to tell him what had happened and that I definitely had gastro and I was crook as a dog.

'I'll come up to your dad's and look after you!' he said. 'But would you be able to pick me up from the train station? I can be there in half an hour.'

Madly doing mental calculations about whether I could make it the ten minutes to the train station and the ten minutes home, I figured I'd be able to do it.

At this point, it was all coming out of my mouth. And SO MUCH had come out of my mouth that my calculations not only included time constraints, but volume limitations. Like, surely there was no more in there that could fucking come out of my body?

So I waited around the house and threw up as much as possible before leaving to pick up Taubs, and had one more shower before popping on a gorgeous loose T-shirt dress. With a flannel on my head and massive bottle filled with water, I drove carefully down to the train station and, thankfully, timed it perfectly. Just as I pulled up, the train was pulling away from the station and everyone was walking off the platform towards the bus zone and the carpark, where I was sitting.

Feeling like pure shit, I was still so grateful to see Taubs' smiling face. He opened the door with a sympathetic smile on his face, took one look at me and gently said, 'Hey sweetie.'

As I was about to respond, I realised that ten minutes without vomiting was probably the limit. I threw the driver-side door open and, with my seatbelt still on, I jerked my head out the door so I could throw up onto the bitumen.

It turned out that my body had decided this was the moment that the diarrhoea was also going to start. The force of throwing up and moving my body so quickly forced the poo to come out of my bum. The good news was that there was no vomit in my car. The bad news was that there was poo.

With tears in my eyes, I turned to look at Taubs, and said, 'Oh my God, I just shat myself.'

And he just rubbed my back and said, 'I know, sweetie.'

Now what?

Not a lie—a genuine question. I've spent a year writing this book. A year where things have happened and I've thought to myself, 'Oh! That will go in the book!' or said, 'Hey, that's a great title idea!' and they haven't made the cut. And other things have happened where I've thought, 'There's no way that's going in the book,' but they've wormed their way in.

Since writing this, I feel like I know myself even better. I wrote from memories that I'd jotted down in a note on my iPhone, but in the process carved out all of this space to feel things I hadn't felt in forever, to create this living memory of who I am and all the things I've experienced, felt, seen and lived.

Before I started writing this, I was so used to sharing things from my life on the podcast or on Instagram, but there is something about immortalising your experiences in a book that is super confronting.

At times, it's been cathartic. There is a living, breathing version of my mum in this book that I am so happy you have been introduced to. Not that my version even holds a candle to the real thing (and don't hold a candle to this book, because you will literally set the pages on fire or melt your Kindle), but I like that there is a perfectly formed version of my mum that lives in here forever now. And long after I'm gone, there will be a living, breathing version of me in here, at the bottom of a 50-cent bin in an op shop.

• • •

You would already have read a chapter (hopefully—maybe you skipped to the end because you got sick of me?) titled 'I'm excited about everything'. At the time I first said it, it was a lie. It was a huge fucking lie and it was a massive disappointment to me when I realised that writing or thinking or saying those words didn't make them true.

I won't lie again.

There are good and bad days. And I'm not excited about everything, but I think I'm getting close. That's true, not just because I wrote the words in here, but because I've followed them up with actions.

I used to think everything would feel better when I got 'there'.

'There', in this example, is the place where you're going, no matter where exactly you're going. The idea of 'there' stays the same, but the actual goal it represents changes constantly. Well, it does for me, anyway.

For me, 'there' has been finishing high school, then getting into uni, then finishing uni, getting my first job, getting my second job, getting my third, fourth and fifth jobs, moving into a bigger house, making more money, making more money and making more money again.

'There' was in a week, in a month or in a year, because by then, surely I'd know what I was supposed to be doing.

'There' has also been when I'm thinner, or when my teeth are straighter, or when my hair is blonder.

'There' was a place where things were easier and I was more confident. Like, 'When I get 1000 followers on Instagram, I'll be so confident about posting all the time—can't wait to get there!' Then it was about how much easier it would be when I got to 10,000 or 50,000 or 100,000 followers. Now that I'm here, as cool as it is, it actually hasn't made that much of a difference.

It's all AWESOME—the only person being fucked over by 'there' is me! I keep moving the goalposts on myself and I don't really know why.

• • •

Not long after Taubs and I began dating officially, he started coming over to have dinner with my family. We were all really close (literally, geographically close—now my siblings and I are spread across Australia), so we'd have dinner once a fortnight or so.

Taubs would always come with me, and one night he complimented Libby on her very fancy kettle. I mean, literally, a kettle. It was a smart kettle, with 300 buttons and many different settings for various types of tea or coffee. You could keep it warm after boiling it and it was just this really fancy kettle that Taubs, who is a big tea drinker, was totally infatuated by.

Last week, I bought the kettle for Taubs. It's been my favourite 'there' I've reached so far.

• • •

Of all the things I ever thought I'd achieve in my life, I don't know that a book was ever on the map. But I guess this is the end of my book.

If you're after an opportunity to take stock of your life, I suggest writing a book. Nothing has made me feel more proud or sad or happy or insanely content.

Every single lie that is in this book is a real lie I've told myself, or others. Every one of them has been part of my life or part of my negative self-talk—thank you for letting me expose myself here and be, pardon the pun, an open book.

The day I started writing this book, I hit play on a Spotify playlist called 'essay writing vibes // study & writing' that had a description reading, 'Let's bang out 1500 words right here right now.' The composer of the playlist was named 'Elizabeth', just like my mum.

So, I spent $169 on a one-off version of Microsoft Word (someone remind me to tell my accountant) and banged out 1500 words. It's actually the first 1500 of this book.

So, to my two muses—my two Elizabeths, my mum and a stranger with a Spotify playlist—thank you.

I can't believe this is my life. And you reading this book means you've helped make it happen, and that's amazing. Thank you.

Lots of love forever and ever,

Toni x

Acknowledgements

I have so many people to thank for helping me make this book come to life. It truly takes a village to create anything, and this book wouldn't be in your hot little hands without these people, just to name a few.

Tessa Feggans, my wonderful book editor extraordinaire. We had so many long Zoom brainstorms that you can see reflected in the pages of this book. Thank you for always making time for me and allowing me to feel heard when I thought there wasn't anything left to give.

And, of course, my new Allen & Unwin family, who put so much faith in my words, story and abilities before they had any proof I could even spell.

Brad March, my manager, for calling me one day and asking, 'Have you ever thought about writing a book?' and making this all happen. I've never had someone put so much blind faith in me—and I say blind faith because you signed me without us ever meeting face to face. I'm very grateful for your guidance and support through my career and also through the very personal pages of this book.

Thank you to all of the friends who I cancelled brunch or dinner plans with when I had a deadline to meet.

To Tim Collins, for being such a special friend who I've laughed and cried with many times over the years, and who has encouraged me to no end at all points of my journey—both personal and professional.

To Paige, for smiling through life with me, both by my side and now, from wherever you are. I miss you very much.

To Étain, for being a creative and passionate friend who will always lend a sensitive ear and has been around for many years. From the days of scraping coins together to afford dinner after going to the footy, or hanging out in the car because we didn't have house keys, there hasn't been a problem I couldn't ask you for advice on. Love ya sick and dead.

To Jase Hawkins, for believing in me from the beginning. I wouldn't have had the opportunities I've had over the years without you pushing me constantly. I've made a special friend in you for life and I'm incredibly grateful.

To Jane, for being supportive and checking on the progress of this book at all times, and making me part of her family. Some of my most special family memories from the past few years are with you: thank you for opening your heart and home to me, and dropping off baked treats in a crisis.

To Jamie, Libby and Hayley, for being a safe space to remember our mum, and for years of special memories that I could never fit into one book.

To Jag, for being the most supportive and loving person, and the best organiser there is. Many laughs and tears both happy and sad have built the foundations of our friendship, and I've never felt embarrassed to express myself to you. You've pushed me when it's been the last thing I've wanted, but the first thing I needed. We've argued like family, but loved like it too, and I couldn't be prouder to have had you by my side for all the challenges and soaring highs that have happened in our lives.

To Lain, for reading, crying and laughing at these words before anyone else got a chance to. For being Toni Lodge's biggest fan and for being such a shining light to the people who know you. For proving to me that love knows no bounds, and that friendships made later in life are just as powerful as ones that have been built over many years. I didn't think anyone could love me as much as my mum did, but you come pretty fucking close. Love you to the ends of the Earth.

A big thank you to the *Toni and Ryan* podcast for giving me space to create and laugh and make memories.

There is no *Toni and Ryan* without the incredible TARPer community—a place where weirdos from all over the world have been able to make friends, laugh and share *harrowing* tales with each other and us.

There is also no *Toni and Ryan* without the Ryan. To Ryan Jon, for being the person I didn't know I was looking for all this time. We all dream of finding someone whose values, goals and excitement levels match our own and I can't believe I found that in you. The hardest worker, worst speller and most caring person I've had the privilege of working with. Everything we've created together has been mind-blowing, and this book wouldn't exist without you.

To my mum. I wouldn't have the courage to walk this Earth without everything you gave me. You're the most incredible woman to ever exist, thank you for being my mum. I love you to the moon and back, and I hope I have made you proud and continue to every day.

To Alex, or Taubs, as he is affectionately known to people around the world. The love of my life and the most supportive, loving and encouraging person in the world. I'm very grateful to you for not only putting up with my loud, garish personality, but also loving it. We've come a long fucking way and I'm so lucky to move through life with you. My Soup Snake, my laugh track, my biggest cheerleader and my favourite way to start and end each day. Of the 7,874,965,825 people in the world and the 129,864,880 books: you're my person, and you're in my book. I love you very much.

And to you! For picking up this book and letting my words fill your brain. I hope they aren't taking up any vital space.